FORGOTTEN GEMS
from
The
Twilight
Zone
Volume 1

FORGOTTEN GEMS

from

The Twilight Zone

A collection of television scripts written by Robert Presnell Jr., William Idelson, E. Jack Neuman, OCee Ritch, John Furia Jr.

Volume 1

Edited by
Andrew Ramage

BearManor Media
2005

Forgotten Gems from The Twilight Zone

© 2005 Andrew Ramage

All Rights Reserved.
Reproduction in whole or in part without the author's permission is strictly forbidden.

Published in the USA by BearManor Media

For information, address:

BearManor Media
P. O. Box 71426
Albany, GA 31708

bearmanormedia.com

Typesetting and layout by John Teehan

Library of Congress Cataloging-in-Publication Data

Forgotten Gems From The Twilight Zone: A Collection of Television Scripts, edited by Andrew Ramage.
p. cm.
ISBN 978-1-62933-137-9

1. Science fiction plays, American. 2. Fantasy drama, American. 3. Television plays, American. 4. American drama--20th century. I. Ramage, Andrew. II. Twilight zone (Television program)

PS627.S39F67 2005
791.45'72--dc22
2004029739

ISBN—978-1-62933-137-9

For Lynne Soto-Seelig

who taught me the importance of good writing

CONTENTS

Acknowledgements i

Foreword 1

"Pattern For Doomsday" by Charles Beaumont 5

"The Chaser" by Robert Presnell, Jr. 13

"Long Distance Call" by William Idelson 51

"The Trouble With Templeton" by E. Jack Neuman 83

"Dead Man's Shoes" by OCee Ritch 123

"I Dream of Genie" by John Furia, Jr. 155

Afterword by Tony Albarella 223

About the Editor 225

ACKNOWLEDGEMENTS

My sincerest thanks goes out to a number of people who helped make this project possible:

To Tony Albarella. Thank you for your invaluable friendship and high regard for Rod Serling's legacy, and for writing the Afterword of this book. To Jeff Zentner, for your ideas and enthusiasm. To Marc Moser—thanks for your constant generosity, and your encyclopedic knowledge of TV and movies.

To Phil Hendrie and our mutual friends Bobbie and Steve Dooley of The Western Estates Homeowners Association in the San Fernando Valley, Mavis Hallandale Leonard of Joyful Union Congregation in Bellflower, and Chris Norton of Redondo Beach, for making me laugh at times when I needed to laugh the most.

To George Clayton Johnson. I thank you, George, for sharing your countless insights with us, not only with your episodes for the series, but for pioneering the publication of sci-fi TV scripts in book form. To William F. Nolan. Thank you, Bill, for supporting this project from the very beginning and for giving me valuable advice and information.

To Chris Conlon, writer extraordinaire, for being gracious enough to proofread this book. Chris and I discussed the possibilities of someone doing this project for about two years before he one day said to me, "I wonder why you don't just do this thing yourself?!"

To John Furia and Bill Idelson, for letting me bring your work out into the light after all these years of being boxed up in the dark. To Mrs. Marian Collier Neuman and Mrs. Marsha Hunt Presnell for generously granting permission to publish your spouses' work.

To James Sheldon, Bill Mumy, and Del Reisman for your colorful remembrances.

To my parents, Andrew Sr. and Faith, for no end of devotion and for not raising me on television…but for picking up cable TV during my first year of college, so I could finally see all the classic TV I'd missed.

Most importantly, to my publisher, Ben Ohmart, who agreed to release this book. Thank you, Ben, for your devotion to this and so many other rarities that would otherwise remain in oblivion.

And last but certainly not least, to Rod Serling, who gave joy to millions with that so-called "think show." This writer opened up new vistas for us all on the night of October 2nd, 1959, and the world has never been the same since. He was more than the unofficial Father of Television—he was a visionary. I think the great director Ted Post said it best about Rod: "He saw the invisible, he felt the intangible, and achieved the impossible."

Andrew Ramage
September, 2004

FOREWORD

Ordinary people in extraordinary situations, at any time in history and any place in our universe. This was the foundation laid by creator Rod Serling and producer Buck Houghton for the stories that were to be part of *The Twilight Zone*, a phenomenal television anthology which would air on CBS from 1959 to 1964.

By the end of the 1950s, Rod Serling had established himself as one of the several finest writers working in television. He had claimed three Emmys, for "Patterns" (*Kraft Theater,* 1955) and the *Playhouse 90* segments "Requiem for a Heavyweight" (1956) and "The Comedian" (1957). These were highly polished, realistic, dark dramas. Suddenly, Serling made an odd decision—he wanted to do series television, with the idea for a new series called *The Twilight Zone*. But the choice was doubly curious. What Serling proposed for the show was unlike anything that had ever been seen on television, which was still a relatively new medium. The show's proposed format didn't go over well at first. Few understood it, most importantly the network that would air it and the sponsors who would underwrite it. This was at the time when advertising agencies were taking their stranglehold of television networks with the mandate of, 'we underwrite your show, you plug our products—you scratch our back, and we'll decide in due course if we want to keep scratching yours.'

Serling was most at home with stories centered around human relationships, often in the form of one or two-character studies with supporting characters. He also tackled commentary on prevalent social issues with great success. Needless to say, the higher-ups at the show's sponsoring corporations were wary of this kind of program being associated with their products. If *The Twilight Zone* was going to be successful and have a significant run, it had to have a different kind of story that covertly tackled such issues as prejudice and intercultural relations, under the guises of fantasy and the surreal. This proved to be a good modus operandi. The finest episodes were unforgettable and the average ones were often far better than most other series' best.

The Twilight Zone went on to offer some of the finest writing ever before or since seen on television, along with some of the finest acting and directing. Soon-to-become legendary talents including Elizabeth Montgomery, Ted Knight, Ron Howard, Martin Landau, and Robert Redford did some of their first work on the show. Long-established figures such as Ida Lupino, Gig Young, Richard Conte, Howard Duff, and Franchot Tone became the presenters of these most sophisticated tales that aired every week for five seasons. The show caught on with its original audiences. It was never a ratings blockbuster, but people liked it. It was fresh, new, innovative. The words 'Twilight Zone' became a part of our vernacular, and the creator himself one-upped his deadpan TV cousin Alfred Hitchcock. Serling became a cultural icon as he stormed the stage, introducing the stories in ways that drew the audience in like a high-gauss magnet.

In the past ten years, the series has seen a resurgence in our popular culture. It endures in reruns and holiday marathons on The SciFi Channel®, Internet websites, memorabilia, and distinguished get-togethers featuring actors, writers, and directors who worked on the series.

When CBS picked up the series in 1959 and in subsequent seasons, it was contractually stated that Serling would contribute the largest share of the scripts. This was obviously a formidable undertaking, even for such a prolific writer who seemed to have ideas bubbling out of him like a geyser. He couldn't possibly furnish ideas for all the stories and have *The Twilight Zone* retain a consistent level of quality from week to week. Buck Houghton, who was assigned by then-CBS president William Self to produce the series, agreed with Serling that Charles Beaumont and Richard Matheson could easily carry most of what would remain. Both had published dozens of short stories that could easily be adapted into television episodes.

On occasion, Serling and the producers bought scripts by other writers. Their stories encompassed similar themes and usually fit *The Twilight Zone* mold quite well. The writing was just as impacting—in some cases more so—as the work of the Serling-Beaumont-Matheson core triad.

The purpose of this book and many television script books, although often unstated, is to present the stories as literary works—a collection of dramatic plays, if you will. Words on paper are often more lucid than the episode as it appears on the TV screen. Often times, valuable material is omitted or altered during shooting due to budgetary limitations and the hubbub of fast-paced production, and thus becomes lost to history. Commentary on what was ultimately filmed is included as well. Stage directions are included, if the writer included them in his script.

While not a strikingly original set of stories, they remain *sui generis* in the way they were *told*.

The bill of faire for this volume includes "The Chaser," a fable about a man who gets the love he desires, and much more, thanks to a certain potion; "Long Distance Call," a horror story about a little boy whose grandmother dies on his birthday and gives him a toy telephone so he can continue to communicate with her; "The Trouble With Templeton," a tale of an aging actor who takes a short trip back in time and as a result, is able to continue his work on Broadway at the moment when he's sure he's been put out to pasture; "Dead Man's Shoes," concerning a homeless gentleman who finds some shiny new shoes, steps into them, and consequently assumes the soul of their previous owner; "I Dream of Genie," which tells of a dullard office worker who gets a chance to move up in the world; and a smaller bonus item, an outline for an unproduced episode titled "Pattern for Doomsday" by Charles Beaumont.

In the following pages, you will be introduced to the work of a unique group of talents who wrote these stories, each a fine storyteller in his own right. As you read their stories, you will see each of their visions and how they contribute to the symmetry and asymmetry of the land of shadow and substance, of things and ideas…the place we've come to know as *The Twilight Zone*.

CHARLES BEAUMONT
"Pattern For Doomsday"

Charles Beaumont (1929-1967) had a writing career that spanned a short fifteen years until it was cut short by early Alzheimer's disease. Beaumont wrote scripts for twenty-two episodes of *The Twilight Zone*, which were recently published (*The Complete Twilight Zone Scripts of Charles Beaumont*, edited by Roger Anker, Gauntlet Press, 2004). He also wrote several scripts and stories for the series that, for any number of reasons, were not produced. Film connoiseurs know Beaumont for "The Wonderful World of The Brothers Grimm," "The Intruder," and "The Seven Faces of Dr. Lao."

Had he survived, Beaumont would have shared an iconoclastic plane with any of the greatest screenwriters of the twentieth century.

Rod Serling created the series, but Charles Beaumont lived in his own personal *Twilight Zone*. The average viewer readily recognizes the thematic threads that run through Rod Serling's *Twilight Zone* episodes. Serling's stories always had a certain amount of sentiment and evoked sympathy for the characters. Serling led a fast-paced life in Hollywood and, often as a form of therapy, wrote of the worn, tired man, or the down-and-out man who gets another chance at glory.

Beaumont's stories were different. He was the only writer on the show who was completely in sync with the great unknown and the uncertainties and question marks that accompany it, the main idea that Serling predicated the series upon. Like any good writer, Beaumont wrote from whence he came. Beaumont's most memorable stories were tales about the darker realms of existence that probed the depths of the extraordinary.

Beaumont had experiences in his life that were frightening to the point where he was able to successfully take what he was feeling and work it into riveting, often tension-packed stories. Thanks to fine directors and actors, they emerged as markedly emotionally-involving episodes of television.

The following is an outline for "Pattern for Doomsday." It was handed over to Jerry Sohl, who expanded it into a full script (recently published in

Filet of Sohl, edited by Christopher Conlon, BearManor Media, 2004), and Cayuga Productions bought it in 1963. It was in the production pipeline, but ultimately never produced. Those familiar with the 1951 George Pal film *When Worlds Collide* or *Deep Impact* (1998) will readily recognize the story, although the basic idea goes back at least a full century to short stories by H.G. Wells and others. It seems appropriate that this piece from the most 'Zonish' of *Twilight Zone* writers, while not entirely original, open this collection.

PATTERN FOR DOOMSDAY

Teaser

The scene is the office of the President of the United States, and at the moment the people there – the President, Chief of Staff General Sinclair, aides, secretaries and Dr. Timothy Randolph – are silent and grave as a projected film they watch ends. The film is that of an object in space as big as the moon which is moving toward the earth at a terrific speed.

Dr. Randolph tells them they are going to die, the world is going to die, for this enormous, jagged hunk of matter is on a collision course with earth and there is no way to stop it.

Is there no margin of error? No. The trajectory of the object has been closely calculated by Dr. Randolph and astronomers all over the world. There is no chance there will be a near-miss. It will strike the earth head-on in six days. There is no way to stop it.

General Sinclair points out there is one chance of escape, but only for eight persons. The new nuclear-powered spaceship, the Varuna II, which has been built for solar system exploration, stands ready in New Mexico. It is up to the President to decide whether it will be used.

The President thinks it should be used. He is told only two crewmen are needed. These and six others could carry on the human race on some distant planet. But who should the six people be?

Everyone looks at the President.

It seems to me, General Sinclair says, that that ought to be up to you, Mr. President.

The President nods solemnly. His face shows the terrible responsibility of making such a decision.

Act 1

At the New Mexico spaceport, people mill back and forth in front of the main gate bearing plaques and posters decrying the fact that only six people, in addition to the two crewmen, will be able to leave earth. Some suggest a lottery; others suggest that everyone be doomed, that no one be spared. Still others proclaim the unfairness of everything.

The loudest of all is rabble rouser Joe Blaylock, who rants and raves about any man playing God. Why not us? Why not you and me? We paid for the Varuna II, we have a right to ride it to safety, he says.

The President arrives with his aides, General Sinclair, and others. Guards hold back the crowd as his car moves in through the gates. The ship is scheduled to take off the next morning.

Captain Gerald Vickers, an officer of about 35, who looks longingly at the ship, tells the President he is grateful to General Sinclair for choosing him for the job of piloting the ship, but he feels guilty about being selected when there are so many men who are better qualified.

The President cuts him short, saying there isn't time for regrets or guilty feelings, Vickers was chosen on the basis of his record, he isn't married, and he's a stable personality, a prime requirement for any colonist. The only question is, can he be equal to the job?

Vickers says firmly he is. With the ship's nuclear resources there won't be any trouble, they can go to Mars, Venus, the other planets and even to Alpha Centauri, the nearest star system with planets, if necessary. Is there food enough to take them that far? Yes, palatable breads, soups, meats and even ice cream can be made from the continuously growing tanks of chlorella, a fast growing single-celled plant. A control group has subsisted on it for a year without ill effects.

Has Vickers chosen his crewman? He has, and he calls over Robert McKenna, a young man of 25, who salutes smartly, says he is happy to be able to accompany the President and his party into outer space in view of what is going to happen in three days. The President tells him he isn't going. McKenna is shocked. He wets his lips nervously and asks why, with escape open to him, the President would rather stay and die. The President smiles wryly and says his wife might not like it if he deserted her. But your wife, McKenna starts to say, but a clamor at the gates draws their attention.

A man is climbing over the wall. He is warned to stay back, but he screams he isn't going to stay and die. He jumps down on this side; three guards overpower him, lead him away. They are taunted by Blaylock and his followers.

In the office that has been set up for the President at the spaceport, which overlooks the Varuna II on her pad, he receives word there is world-wide rioting as a result of the nearness of doomsday. He arranges to address the country again for a final time in an effort to reduce hysteria. A call from Dr. Randolph imparts the information the stellar mass is unchanged; it is still headed straight for earth and nothing is in its way.

The President summons Capt. Vickers, indicates six folders, the dossiers on the six people he has chosen to continue humanity's heritage on an unknown world. He explains that they are all fertile, are all in good physical condition and all have special attributes that render then prime choices for the journey.

A buzzer informs him that the six have arrived. He instructs that they be sent in one at a time.

The six who come in are divergent types, all with contrasting personalities and views. They are:

Dr. Russell Conrad, 42, a psychiatrist, who was a fine physician and surgeon before he entered the field of psychiatry and made a name for himself. He is a widower. His view is that humanity has a problem of survival, that he has been selected seems natural (without his seeming to be an egotist) and he's already made the adjustment, said his farewells.

Connie Clark, 28, a wire services correspondent and Pulitzer prizewinner, who will record everything that happens. She is pretty, confident, excited. She is sorry for those who are not escaping, but she considers this the biggest and most fortuitous assignment of her life.

Lili Wong, 30, Eurasian practicing attorney. Quiet, brilliant, willing to accept death, if necessary. She will set up the rules for behavior and will advise the group on the administration of justice.

Jody Hallam, 30, Negro composer. There's going to be a great need for music and Hallam will carry all the great music in his head and write it again for the generations to follow, after the colony is established. He hopes he'll prove worthy of the trust placed in his memory, feels that someone must make sure that the great music is not destroyed.

Dr. Regina Walsh, 35, eminent woman biologist, also well known for her work in ecology and a dabbler in art. She had never expected to be able to apply her knowledge to new life forms and an alien environment. She is sorry that the life of earth had not been completely mastered before it and all of the people on it were destroyed.

Dr. Phillip Jewell, 50, world-famed philosopher, whose wisdom and experience will aid the group as they start life anew; he will help evaluate what is being done, will draw on his career.

But Dr. Jewell says he doesn't want to go. The President and the others are shocked. Why doesn't the President go in his place? The President explains about not letting anyone married go. Jewell says he is married – married to the human race. He cannot leave it.

Act 2

Dr. Jewell heatedly declares that he can better serve humanity by dying with it, being a part of its final agonies. Is it fair that he should be chosen to survive the coming holocaust? By what right should he still live when billions will die? And what right has anyone to decide this?

There is argument, the others assuring him he is wrong, as long as there is a chance for survival, even if it is survival for only eight, humanity ought to take it. Isn't survival an instinct? What is wrong with you, Doctor?

The President takes Jewell to the wide window where they see the people gathered, their faces pressed to the chain link fence, eyeing the spaceship longingly. Each one of them would take Jewell's place, but each has not proved himself to be the man Jewell is.

Why not take one of them? Jewell asks. All men are equal, Mr. President; you've said that yourself.

True, the President says. So in that case it doesn't make any difference and you are as logical a choice as the next man. Therefore, by my last executive order, you will be on that ship whether you like it or not. There is no more time for argument.

Jewell looks around. He can't argue with that. He smiles wanly. He will go as long as the choice is not his to make.

Good, the President says. Now Capt. Vickers will issue you your instructions and then you can all have your last night's sleep on earth.

Morning. The group assembles outside the spaceport building with their belongings, limited by weight and size. They are being weighed.

Joe Blaylock and his well-wishers jeer and taunt the assembled passengers. Rocks are thrown.

The group inside is greeted by the President and his aides and General Sinclair. He informs them he has just heard from Dr. Randolph; the object hurtling toward earth is much nearer now. No change in trajectory. It has finally entered the solar system.

The President is speaking a few last words when a car runs to and crashes through the gate, machine-gunning guards left and right. It swerves, narrowly misses the group ready for flight, swerves again and veers off toward the spaceship. Guards commence firing at it. The ship is only a hundred feet away when the car goes out of control and crashes. But Joe Blaylock jumps out, runs for and gets in the ship, shouting that if he can't go, then nobody goes. He disappears inside. There is an explosion, wrecking the interior and blowing a hole in the ship. Blaylock staggers out, falls dead on the platform.

Everyone has watched, horrified. The ship is ruined. Now no one will get away. There is no time for repairs. The crowd at the gate begins to disperse. They will return to their homes to face the calamity there.

The President speaks to the group. They might as well return to their homes. He will provide jets to take each one wherever he wishes to meet his end. As for himself, he will return to Washington to his wife.

An aide runs out with an emergency message. The President answers by going to a nearby car and picking up the phone there. His eyes light up as he hears the message.

Dr. Randolph is excitedly telling him that the gravitational forces encountered when the mass entered the solar system has torn it apart. It has literally exploded into five pieces; they are spreading out and will miss the earth by many thousands of miles.

The President recounts this information as the body of Joe Blaylock is carried by.

They all look at Blaylock.

Though the whole earth had been endangered, the man who swore no one would escape is the only one who was the victim of it.

THE END

ROBERT PRESNELL, Jr.
"The Chaser"

Robert Presnell, Jr. (1914-1986) wrote for such shows as *Studio One, The Virginian, McCloud* and *Banacek,* in addition to a number of TV movies and several minor-league feature films. For over 40 years, he was married to silver screen actress Marsha Hunt.

Originally written for *The Billy Rose Television Theater* in 1951 and based on a short story by John Collier, Presnell expanded "The Chaser" significantly for *The Twilight Zone.* Collier's story is a two-character piece with only a mention of the main character's love interest. She is never heard from or seen, and the lone setting is in a certain wise man's home. The basic story itself is an ancient one. Man loves woman, but woman despises man. Man summons magic potion to get her to love him but it works too well and now he can't get rid of her. He obtains yet another potion to undo the spell, but the plans run amok and now he's stuck with her for good.

Cast in the lead of the television episode was future Emmy and Tony Award winner George Grizzard. While he never became a household name, Grizzard was one of Hollywood's most reliable actors at the time. He started in the 1950s on Broadway; his performances were hailed as exceptional and he soon began working in TV and film. "The Chaser" marked the first of two performances Grizzard made on the series, and he gives a competently controlled performance as the boyish Roger. Three seasons later, Grizzard returned to *The Twilight Zone* for the starring role in Beaumont's "In His Image," in which he had a far more Herculean task, playing both an inventor who creates an artificial man, and the artificial man himself. Character actress Patricia Barry, whose career in television, film, and theater spans more than five decades, co-starred as Leila. But the finest of the three characterizations is John McIntire's Professor Daemon, which remains the central force of the piece. Using gruff vocal inflection, well-modulated with a pedantic elegance, he makes the character come alive. McIntire appeared in over forty feature films in the 1950s, although he is perhaps best known for his appearance as a bristly sheriff in Hitchcock's "Psycho," which he portrayed right around the time he worked on *The Twilight Zone.*

Most impressive of "The Chaser" as a TV episode is its visual appeal. The sets are superbly designed—Leila's posh apartment and the library/home of Professor Daemon, featuring bookshelves which stood over 15 feet high. Appropriately enough, music from Tchaikovsky's version of "Romeo and Juliet" plays in the background during one of the sequences with Roger and Leila. Trademark *Twilight Zone* moments come at the end, when Leila reports that the latest death in the rabbit hutch is hers. Feeling guilty, Roger undergoes a Freudian slip of sorts; he drops the glass of laced champagne as he gets the news that fatherhood is imminent. Realizing that he's destined to a life of being doted on and fawned over, he mumbles a pathetic, "I could never have gone through with it!", and promptly faints. Quick glance out to the patio, where we see Daemon's doppelganger sitting comfortably in a lawn chair, smoking a cigar. He blows a ring of smoke, morphed into the shape of a heart, which fades up into the stars. In retrospect, this seems a wise alteration from the more abrupt ending originally written by Presnell.

Douglas Heyes directed eight episodes of *The Twilight Zone* anthology, including "The Chaser." Heyes was a skilled leader who could always be counted on to unleash the magic in fantasy stories, which included some of the finest in the series—"The Howling Man" starring H.M. Wynant and John Carradine, "Nervous Man in a Four Dollar Room" starring Joe Mantell, "The After Hours" starring Anne Francis, and "Eye of the Beholder" starring Maxine Stuart. In all of these, he created the unforgettable, bringing out the best in literally every element of production. "The Chaser" did not have the knotty complexities that Heyes usually surmounted with aplomb, but it stands on its own as a classic vignette with a valid take-home lesson: don't try to get others to love you. Even if you momentarily succeed, they will certainly come back to haunt you later!

"The Chaser" was originally broadcast on 13 May, 1960.

THE CHASER

CAST

ROGER SHACKLEFORTH	an impressionable, romantic young man
LEILA	a lovely girl
HOMBURG	middle aged, imperious, and very impatient
BLONDE) FAT LADY) TALL MAN)	typical New Yorkers at phone scene
PROFESSOR DAEMON	a demon

SETS

EXTERIOR	A street corner in Greenwich Village —Scene 23, 24 Street outside Roger's apartment – for Tag of Act I & II
INTERIOR	Drugstore at phone booth Leila's apartment Professor Daemon's study, vestibule and exterior faced street door Bar – in the Village. Probably dimly lit and intimate

ACT ONE
FADE ON:

1. SHOT (ART) OF AN ODD LOOKING SKY

With strange clouds that drift across the sky. PAN DOWN for LONG ANGLE SHOT of a road that stretches out across a barren landscape punctuated by odd rock croppings and an occasional gnarled-branched tree. The CAMERA STARTS MOVING DOWN this road at a fast clip heading toward a far out horizon. Over this we hear a Narrator's Voice.

> NARRATOR'S VOICE
> This highway leads to the shadowy tip of reality; a through route to the land of the different, the bizarre, the unexplainable.
> (a pause)
> You go as far as you like on this road. Its limits are only those of the mind itself. Ladies and gentlemen, you're entering the wondrous dimension of imagination. Next stop –

At this moment we've reached the end of the road and are just a moment away from what appears to be a precipice leading out into nothingness. Concurrent with the next line of narration the lettering springs up in front of the camera almost as if on a hinge.

> NARRATOR'S VOICE
> *The Twilight Zone!*

The CAMERA MOVES through into the lettering smashing it into bits and then continuing on through until we are suspended in night sky. A SLOW PAN DOWN to opening shot of the play.

2. INT INSERT SECTION OF A SMALL DRUGSTORE WITH ONE PHONE BOOTH

The door is closed and three people are standing in line, waiting their turn. The first is a fat lady with packages, the second is a thin man with glasses, and the third is a pretty blond with everything. Each has her and his reason for impatience, and each evinces it by peering into the closed phone booth. We peer in too, and see Roger Shackleforth sitting disconsolately, the receiver at his ear.

3.   REVERSE ANGLE THE WAITING PEOPLE ROGER'S P.O.V.

They are all looking at him with impersonal malice. We hear the busy signal that Roger is listening to. We see him hang up. The waiting people move expectantly. Roger takes the coin out of the return slot and sadly puts it in above and dials again. The waiting line sags unhappily. Over this shot of Roger we hear the Narrator's voice.

> NARRATOR'S VOICE
> Mr. Roger Shackleforth. Age, youthful twenties. Occupation—being in love. Not *just* love—but madly, passionately, illogically, miserably, all-consumingly in love…with a young woman named Leila who has a vague recollection of his face and even less than a passing interest. In a moment you'll see a switch because Mr. Roger Shackleforth, the young gentleman so much in love, will take a short, but very meaningful journey into The Twilight Zone!

FADE TO BLACK:

OPENING BILLBOARD
FIRST COMMERCIAL
FADE ON:

4.   INT INSERT DRUGSTORE PHONE BOOTH LONG SHOT OVER THE HEADS OF THE WAITING LINE LOOKING TOWARD ROGER

Still on the phone. An important looking man who somehow carries the distinctions of another era rushes in. He is wearing a black homburg and a chesterfield coat and a boulevardier mustache perhaps. He is immediately disconcerted by the waiting line. He looks into the phone booth, then at those waiting.

5.   MED GROUP SHOT

> HOMBURG
> This is madness. It's becoming impossible to make a phone call anywhere in New York.

                    BLONDE
You can say that again.

                    HOMBURG
Thank you. As it happens I have an emergency.

                    FAT LADY
                 (with packages)
We all got emergencies.

                    HOMBURG
You can't all have emergencies. I beg of you, let
me go in next. I can't tell you how important it is.

                    FAT LADY
After me.

                    TALL MAN
After me.

                    BLONDE
After me.

                    HOMBURG
It's a plot. Every time I want to phone, ten
thousand people run to all the available phone
booths and stand there. I've tried every drug
store and cigar store in blocks.

6.   REVERSE ANGLE ROGER'S P.O.V.

From inside booth looking out over Roger's profile toward the waiting line.
Once again he's listening to a busy signal which can be heard o.s. He sighs
deeply, his thin, sensitive, very idealistic face a study in sadness. He hangs up
once more. The waiting line looks anticipatory, but Roger sighs and deposits
the coin again and begins to dial.

7.   DIFFERENT ANGLE OUTSIDE THE LINE

                    HOMBURG
This is an outrage. He's making another call!

                    FAT LADY
            It's only his fifth.

                    BLONDE
            He don't even talk. He just dials. Maybe he's got
            a dialect, huh?

                    HOMBURG
            I simply cannot stand this.
                    (he pulls out his wallet, extracts
                    several bills)
            I must go next. I will buy your place.
                    (to the blonde)
            A dollar for your place.

                    BLONDE
            Sold.

He pays her. She steps back a little. Homburg moves to the man, holding out a dollar. The man accepts and steps back. Homburg moves to the fat lady.

                    FAT LADY
            Why should first place be the same as third.
            Two dollars.

                    HOMBURG
            Two dollars.

He pays it and steps in front of her, now concentrating all his attention on Roger. He perhaps hopes he can think him out of the booth.
                                            CUT TO:

8.   MED CLOSE SHOT ROGER

His face brightens and we hear a girl's voice say hello. Roger almost faints in ecstasy at the sound of it. He tries to say something, but for a moment the words just don't come out.

                                            CUT TO:

9.   INT LEILA'S APARTMENT LEILA ON PHONE

                    LEILA
               (with charm)
        Hello…?
                                        CUT TO:

10.   CLOSE SHOT ROGER

                    ROGER
        Hello, Leila darling, it's Roger.

11.   CLOSE SHOT LEILA

                    LEILA
               (charm diminished)
        Oh, hello, Roger, what is it?
                                        CUT TO:

12.   CLOSE SHOT ROGER

                    ROGER
        May I come to see you?
                                        CUT TO:

13.   CLOSE SHOT LEILA

                    LEILA
        I can't. I couldn't bear to see anyone now.
        I'm a mess.
               (She is not.)
                                        CUT TO:

14.   CLOSE SHOT ROGER

                    ROGER
               (gestures as he talks)
        You could never be a mess. Listen, Leila, I have
        to see you. Have to. If I don't see you I'll…burst,
        or something. Please have dinner with me.

                    LEILA'S VOICE
               (filtered)
        I can't, I told you I've got a date. And I can't talk
        now, I have to dress.

                    ROGER
　　All right, a cocktail. At least have a cocktail with me.

                    LEILA'S VOICE
                    (filtered)
　　No, Roger, it's impossible.

                    ROGER
　　Then let me come up for just a moment. I must
　　see you, darling, must…furiously, fiercely, must.
　　I love you.
                                        CUT TO:

15.　　CLOSE SHOT LEILA

                    LEILA
                    (her voice brittle with distaste and
                    total boredom)
　　Roger, I don't want to be rude. I'm not a rude
　　person by nature, but why don't you get lost?
　　I've got a date and I have to dress. Why don't you
　　find a nice schoolteacher or social worker or…or
　　like that and leave me alone!
                                        CUT TO:

16.　　CLOSE SHOT ROGER

                    ROGER
　　Well, then let me just come and sit in your
　　apartment. I just want to be near you…

                    LEILA'S VOICE
                    (filtered)
　　Roger, stop this. You're acting like a baby. I can't
　　see you now, and that's that.

                    ROGER
　　Than talk to me. Just say something to me…
　　anything…
                                        CUT TO:

17.　　CLOSE SHOT LEILA

                          LEILA
            (her eyes close, she heaves a huge, deep sigh)
        Say something? All right, Roger, I'll say something.
        Why don't you take a flying jump at the moon!

She slams the receiver down.
                                                CUT TO:

18.   TWO SHOT ROGER

As he sits there numbly and disconsolately and the Homburg who opens the
door and leans in.

                         HOMBURG
        There, now, you've finished haven't you?

                          ROGER
        She hung up on me. I've got to call her back just
        once more and make sure she isn't sore at me.

                         HOMBURG
        No, no, please, I have an emergency.

                          ROGER
        So have I.

He starts to put in the coin again.

                         HOMBURG
        No, it won't do any good to call her. I understand
        your problem, I heard you through the door. You
        can't solve it on the telephone. Here...
                (he reaches into his pocket and pulls
                out some cards, shuffles through them,
                and hands one to Roger)
        Here is the way to solve your problem. It's the
        only way. Go see this man. Go see him. Right now.

Roger takes the card and reads it. Homburg reaches in and helps Roger to
come out.

                            HOMBURG
            Believe me, there is no other way. I know. Go see
            that man and he will help you. Excuse me.
                      (he gets Roger out and gets himself
                       into the booth)
            Go and see him now and your problems will be
            solved before the day is over.
                      (he nods, closing the door)
            Thank you. Emergency!

Roger stands, mouth slightly ajar, and he looks again at the card.

                                                    CUT TO:

19.   EXTREMELY TIGHT CLOSE SHOT THE CARD

        It reads, "Professor A. Daemon, 22 Bank Street, New York City"

20.   CLOSE SHOT ROGER

        As he reads aloud.

                              ROGER
            Professor A. Daemon, 22 Bank Street, New York City.

He looks up from the card, puzzled.

21.   REVERSE ANGLE LOOKING TOWARD WAITING LINE

        Who stare at him.

22.   CLOSE SHOT ROGER

As he looks at them embarrassed, stuffs the card in his pocket and goes down the line, exiting.

22.   DIFFERENT ANGLE THE LINE

As each looks at the other, resuming their vigil as when we found them, peering expectantly toward the booth.

                    BLONDE
        Emergency, huh? What type emergency do you
        think it is?

                    MAN
        If third place is a dollar, and first place two dollars,
        I should have gotten at least a dollar and a half.

They peer and wait

                                        DISSOLVE TO:

23.   EXT STREET CORNER FULL SHOT

As Roger stands there looking up at a street sign which reads, "Bank Street". He takes out the card and looks at it again.

24.   CLOSE SHOT THE CARD

                                        LAP DISSOLVE TO:

25.   SAME CARD

It is shown on the door of a house. Roger stands there. He raises his hand to ring the bell, drops it. Raises it, then with a what-can-I-lose gesture, he rings. He waits, tempted to run. The door slowly opens and he hesitates, then goes in. He looks to each side and behind the door and finds no one. There was no buzz.

26.   INT SMALL VESTIBULE WITH ANOTHER DOOR AT THE
        FAR END

This one slowly opens too. Roger sidles through it.
                                        CUT TO:

27.   INT STUDY OF PROFESSOR DAEMON

This is a room made of books. A whole wall of them going behind the desk. There are piles of them on the floor and on the desk with no other furniture visible. Professor Daemon is behind the desk wearing an eye shade, a kind of puckered face, gnome-like little man who has kind of a perpetual dour smile.

                    DAEMON
        Come in, come in. Stop skulking at the door
        and come in.

ROGER
I wasn't skulking. I just didn't know if...

DAEMON
A common enough disease, not knowing if.
Sit on that pile of books there.
  (indicating)
Now let's see, do I know you?

ROGER
No sir. As a matter of fact . . .

DAEMON
Umm. Then you haven't come for a bottle of the Glove Cleaner.

ROGER
Glove Cleaner? No. As a matter of fact...

DAEMON
Too bad. Well, perhaps another time.

ROGER
As a matter of fact...

DAEMON
You keep saying that. Come to the point.

ROGER
The point is that I'm not sure why I came at all. You see, a man gave me your card. A stranger.

DAEMON
Satisfied former customer, quite likely.

ROGER
I don't really know why I came though. I was in a phone boo...

DAEMON
Of course you know why you came. No one comes to see me without a purpose.

ROGER
But I don't even know what kind of a doctor you are...

DAEMON
Ointments, salves, powders, sovereign remedies, nectars, lotus blossoms, tonics, toxins, anti-toxins, decoctions, concoctions and potions. All guaranteed.

ROGER
But I don't need anything like that.

DAEMON
You must. You're here.

ROGER
Well, I don't really need a doctor.

DAEMON
You certainly need something. You look feverish.

ROGER
Well it's...you know...sort of...nothing.

DAEMON
Nothing? Nothing I don't supply. Something is my specialty. Anything is what you'll get here. You're ambitious? Is that it? You want success, money, admirers, the world at your feet?

ROGER
(interrupting)
No, that's not it.

DAEMON
Power. You want power.

ROGER
You don't understand. All I want is Leila.

DAEMON
(stopped)
Leila?

ROGER
Yes. If I have Leila, I can do all the rest myself.

DAEMON
(depressed)
Leila. I might have known. All he wants is Leila. I offer practically everything, and what does he want? Leila.

ROGER
(making to go)
And I guess there's nothing you can do about it.

DAEMON
That's the simplest of all. That's the elementary parlor-trick of my science. You disappoint me.

ROGER
You don't understand. I love someone named Leila…but she doesn't love me. I don't know why I'm telling you all this…

DAEMON
I do. I can arrange it so she'll love you.

ROGER
How?

DAEMON
(uninterested)
I promise you that she'll never leave your side. When she isn't telling you she loves you, she'll be gazing at you lovingly. She won't even eat until you do, and nothing will be too much for you to ask of her. She'll worship you. She'll beg for your kisses, weep for joy at your touch. And if, in passing time, you should perhaps look at another girl, and even do a little more than look, she'll feel

hurt, but she will forgive you and love you just the
same.
> (a pause as he looks away
> thoughtfully)

Frankly, you'd get the same shake from an affectionate Cocker Spaniel.

28.   CLOSE SHOT ROGER

As he has nodded ecstatically at each new sentence, growing more and more excited. He waves off the Cocker Spaniel line.

ROGER
(breathlessly)
That would be wonderful. That's all in the world I'd want…my Leila's love.

29.   CLOSE SHOT DAEMON

DAEMON
(his eyes roll upwards and he looks
the perfect picture of a desperately
bored man who has heard this song
a hundred million times)
His Leila's love. And if it isn't his Leila's love it's his Dorothy's love or Gwen's love or Rhea's love. Tell me something, are you sure you wouldn't be interested in the Glove Cleaner as I call it?

30.   TWO SHOT

As Daemon opens a drawer and takes out a bottle of clear liquid, sets it on the table. A pretty bottle, decorative like an expensive perfume bottle.

DAEMON (CONT'D)
There are many names for it, including the eradicator. But Glove Cleaner is a nice, non-descriptive title. Clean, colorless, tasteless, unidentifiable and sure.

31.   CLOSE SHOT ROGER

           ROGER
I'm not really interested in glove cleaners.

32.   TWO SHOT

           DAEMON
Why not? It's sure, it's swift, it leaves no traces.
It's perfect for its purpose.

           ROGER
I don't think you're making any sense.

           DAEMON
My boy, that is all I make, which is why I'm such
a lonely man. You're sure you don't want to try the
Glove Cleaner? It's very expensive, you know. I
doubt if you could afford it. This little bottle for
instance, costs a thousand dollars.

           ROGER
A thousand dollars! Are all your prices like that?

           DAEMON
Some are, some aren't.

           ROGER
But the…the thing that will make Leila love me…?

           DAEMON
           (disgustedly)
Oh that.
           (he opens a drawer and takes out an
           ugly, dirty little bottle)
This is only a dollar. Love potions are my cheapest item.

           ROGER
A dollar? A dollar to make Leila love me—and it
won't hurt her.

                    DAEMON
        If it's going to hurt anybody, it'll be you. But I
        don't expect you to believe me. Put it in anything.
        A drink, stew, soup, coffee, water, anything. You'll
        get exactly what you say you want.

33.   CLOSE SHOT BOTTLE OF LOVE POTION

As Roger picks it up. PULL BACK FOR DIFFERENT ANGLE THE
TWO OF THEM.

                    ROGER
        I don't really believe it. But I'll try it. I'll try
        anything. Thank you, Professor Daemon. If this
        works, I'll be the happiest man in the world.

                    DAEMON
                  (simultaneously)
        The happiest man in the world!
                                            DISSOLVE TO:

34.   INT LEILA'S APARTMENT NIGHT SECTION OF LIVING
        ROOM

The doorbell rings and Leila comes from another room to open the door. Roger enters, with flowers and a small bottle of champagne.

35.   FULL SHOT THE ROOM

                    ROGER
        Hello, Leila.

                    LEILA
        Roger what do you want? I told you I was busy
        tonight.

                    ROGER
        Just for a minute. Just for a little minute.
                  (he hands her the flowers)
        Flowers. See?

                    LEILA
               (looking ceilingward)
          That's very nice, Roger. Now if you'll just run
          along…

                    ROGER
          I couldn't have lasted the night without seeing you.
          You don't understand what it's like to love someone,
          to love anyone so much and so desperately.
               (he holds up the bottle)
          Champagne. Just enough for two glasses. That's
          not much to ask, is it? Spare me five minutes and
          have just one drink with me.

                    LEILA
          Roger, you're acting like a clod! A silly, stupid,
          sophomoric clod.

                    ROGER
               (helplessly)
          I love you.

36.   MED CLOSE SHOT LEILA

                    LEILA
          Oh, stop saying that.

37.   MED CLOSE SHOT ROGER

He holds up the bottle, his eyes still pleading.

38.   TWO SHOT

                    LEILA
          Oh, all right. One drink. Five minutes, then
          you go. I'll go put on a dress.

39.   TRACK SHOT ROGER

As he goes over to the bar table.

                    ROGER
            It's like…it's like millennium.

40.   MED CLOSE SHOT LEILA

Who sighs, shakes her head, exits into the other room.

41.   PAN SHOT BACK OVER TO ROGER

Who uncorks the champagne, takes the glasses and fills one and almost fills the other. Then he takes the bottle from his pocket and pours the whole thing in, rubs his hands happily, then calls out.

                    ROGER
            All right, darling?

42.   MOVING SHOT WITH HIM

As he carries the two glasses toward her as Leila comes from her room. He hands Leila the mickey.

                    LEILA
            In addition to being a clod—you have not one
            iota of pride.
                    (she takes the glass)
            Come on, let's get this over with.

                    ROGER
                    (holds up his glass)
            To the moment you fall in love with me. To that
            precious, sweet moment.

                    LEILA
                    (as she sips)
            Don't hang by your earlobes waiting.
                    (she puts down the glass, looks at him
                    for a moment)
            Roger, look little friend, believe me I don't want
            to hurt you, but you mustn't come here anymore.
            You bug me, understand? So don't come here
            anymore.

ROGER
(shrugs)
If that's the way you want it, but I'll never forget you—never!

LEILA
I've got news for you, the reverse is not true!

He watches her as she finishes her drink. She puts the glass down.

LEILA
Your time's up. Thanks for the flowers and the champagne. Now goodbye, Roger.

ROGER
(still watching expectantly)
Excellent champagne, wasn't it?

LEILA
It'll pass. Now what are you looking at me like that for?

ROGER
Perhaps it's my last look!

LEILA
All right, now you've had it. Really. Roger, let's not prolong this, I haven't time anyway. Please go now.

Roger takes her glass and his slowly to the bartable, puts them down, then turns, hesitates, and starts for the door. He is about to give up. He stops beside her.

ROGER
Well, goodbye, Leila.

LEILA
Goodbye, Roger.

She opens the door.

                    ROGER
                  (hopefully)
              One last…little kiss?

                    LEILA
        Ohhhhh this boy! Roger, you're positively
        revolting.

                    ROGER
        But Leila, I'm doing just what you asked me to!
        I may never see you again.

                    LEILA
        You're a fool.

She kisses him quickly and meaningless on the cheek. Roger sags.

                    ROGER
        I didn't mean like that.

                    LEILA
        Roger, I just can't go through this. I've never seen
        anything like you. You're absolutely impossible.
        I don't love you. I don't want you here, I don't
        even like you at this moment. Now please go!

Roger hangs his head and desperately turns his reluctant feet toward the door and grudgingly moves. Leila stops him.

                    LEILA
        Ohhhh…here…

She takes his head in her hands suddenly and kisses him on the mouth, briefly, then pushes him away.

                    LEILA
        That's all I can do…and it took all my strength.

Roger nods, goes to the door and is almost out and she is about to close it, when she hesitates.

                        LEILA
        Roger…

He turns slowly, unhopefully.

                        LEILA
        Wait a minute. Perhaps I'm cruel. I don't mean to be.

                        ROGER
                    (nods)
        I know.

He turns away.

                        LEILA
        Roger…

He turns back to face her. She comes to him.

                        LEILA
        Let me make it nicer.

She kisses him again, on the mouth, more tenderly, and then there is a pause. She looks at him oddly, then reaches up her mouth to kiss him again. Her lips touch his once more and she suddenly throws her arms about his neck and pulls his head fiercely down, making a moaning sound. She kisses him passionately, then staggers back, her hands to her head.

                        LEILA
        Wha-wha-what's happening?

                        ROGER
                    (grinning happily)
        What difference?
                    (and then suddenly he's Jimmy Cagney
                    and Valentino and Gable, he holds out
                    his arms)
        Commere, baby!

Leila hurls herself into them.

43. ANGLE SHOT OVER THEIR SHOULDERS

Looking toward the window facing the street. DOLLY INTO THE window for a long shot looking outside. Down below on the sidewalk underneath a lamppost is Dr. Daemon looking up, smiling quizzically.

FADE TO BLACK

END ACT ONE

ACT TWO

FADE ON:

44. INT LIVING ROOM LEILA'S APARTMENT NIGHT

Much time has passed. Leila looks somewhat less predatory and more domestic. Roger looks harried, like a man who grabbed a lollipop and found a scorpion on the stick. He sits in a chair reading, but is completely aware that Leila is crouched on the floor staring adoringly up at him. He glances down nervously then quickly back to his book which could easily be upside down Arabic for all he knows.

45. TWO SHOT

ROGER
(finally)
Leila…couldn't you please sit in a chair?

LEILA
Yes, my darling husband. I'm sorry if it bothers you. I love to kneel at your feet.

ROGER
Well, kneel in a chair.

LEILA
Which chair, darling?

ROGER
Any chair. It doesn't matter.

LEILA
Do you want your slippers, darling?

ROGER
(patiently)
No thanks. They make my feet hot.

LEILA
If your feet are hot now, I'll put my hands in ice water and then caress…

ROGER
(interrupting)
No, no, my feet are fine.

LEILA
All right.
(pause)
Roger, don't you want to smoke your pipe?

ROGER
It bites my tongue. It isn't broken in very well.

LEILA
I'd be happy to break it in for you. I'll smoke it while you're at the office, then when you come home…

ROGER
No, Leila, thank you, but no thanks.

LEILA
You're welcome.

She sits in a chair and stares at him. Roger tries to avoid the impact of her stare and rummages through his pockets for a cigarette. She leaps up and brings him a box of them, and lights one for him.

LEILA
Here's one, darling. I'm sorry, I should have put the box beside you.

ROGER
Thank you.

LEILA
Shall I rub your back?

ROGER
You just finished rubbing my back.

LEILA
I know, but I adore touching you. If you'd like me to rub it again...

ROGER
No, it's all right. Leila, can't you find something to do...or something?

LEILA
I'm with you, that's all I want to do...be with you.

ROGER
Yes, well, I mean, you've been with me so much... for six months. Wouldn't you like to go to a movie or see some friends or anything?

LEILA
Not without you, dearest.

ROGER
Leila, wouldn't you just once in a while like some time alone?

LEILA
I can hardly endure that when you're at the office. Sometimes I spend the whole afternoon just looking at your picture, or your blue suit hanging on a coat hanger.

ROGER
That's nice. I...ah, don't you think if you developed some sort of hobby...you know... something that would interest you and...

LEILA
I've got news for you. You're my hobby, Roger.

ROGER
(with desperately strained patience)
Leila…I've asked you before…please don't say that. Please don't say, "I've got news for you". That… that does something to my insides. Like a fingernail on a blackboard.

LEILA
It does, sweetheart? I'm sorry. I'll never say it again.
    (pause)
I'm disturbing your reading, aren't I?

ROGER
Oh no, no.

LEILA
Did I disturb you by asking if I disturbed you?

ROGER
    (slipping)
No!
    (hastily controls himself)
No, darling, of course not.
    (but his hands are shaking)

LEILA
I love you, Roger. I'm so happy you're you. You're just perfect. I love to say I love you. I love to love you.

ROGER
    (suddenly stands)
Leila, I have to go out. Out.
    (he laughs a little inanely)
Appointment. Almost forgot. Business. Have to go out.

LEILA
Will you be long?

                    ROGER
            Don't know. May be late.

                    LEILA
                (getting his coat)
            Shall I come too?

                    ROGER
            No, no, you stay here, hug my hat or something.
            I won't be very late.

He snatches his coat from her and goes toward the door, getting it partially on.

                    LEILA
            Is something the matter, Roger darling?

                    ROGER
                (babbling)
            No. Appointment. Late. Air. Have to go out.
            Be back. Appointment. Out.

                    LEILA
            I'll love you even more while you're gone...

Then he goes out the door as she says this.

46.   MOVING SHOT LEILA

As she runs to the window and looks out, waves to Roger and blows kisses.

                                        DISSOLVE TO:

47.   INT BAR NIGHT FULL SHOT THE BAR

A man and woman are sitting on barstools, chummy. Roger comes in without purpose. There is saccharine jukebox music, a love ballad that drips out of the machine. Rogers moves to the bar.

                    BARTENDER
            What'll it be.

                    ROGER
        A drink. Anything. Strong. Double.

                    BARTENDER
        Anything special?

                    ROGER
        Yeah, something special.

The bartender pours a double whiskey. Roger nervously lights a cigarette which is slight crumpled, curving downward. He looks at the couple at the bar who now lean forward and kiss.

48.   REVERSE ANGLE LOOKING TOWARD ROGER THE COUPLE'S POV

Roger shudders.

49.   TWO SHOT ROGER AND THE BARTENDER

                    BARTENDER
        Got troubles?

                    ROGER
        Troubles.

                    BARTENDER
        Dame?

                    ROGER
        If you only knew.

                    THE GIRL
        I love you, David.

                    MAN
        I love you, too.

Roger takes the drink straight, throws the glass over his shoulder, slaps a bill on the bar and walks determinedly away.

                        BARTENDER
                Hey, don't you want your change?

Roger is gone. The bartender shrugs, looks at a five dollar bill and shrugs again as he puts it in the cash register.

                        DISSOLVE TO:

50.   EXT 22 BANK STREET NIGHT MED CLOSE SHOT
        DAEMON'S DOOR

As Roger arrives there and rings. The door opens as before.
CAMERA DOLLIES in with Roger.

51. MOVING SHOT WITH HIM

Through the ante-room and then through the door into Daemon's den.

52.   INT DAEMON'S DEN NIGHT MED CLOSE SHOT ROGER

As he comes in. Suddenly his purpose leaves him and he seems aimless and lacking.

53.   TWO SHOT THE TWO MEN

                          ROGER
                Oh, hello, Professor Daemon.

                          DAEMON
                Ah yes. I've been expecting you.

                          ROGER
                You have? Well yes, I rather thought you might
                like to hear how things turned out.

                          DAEMON
                I know how they turned out.

                          ROGER
                That potion certainly worked.

                          DAEMON
                        (wearily)
                I know, I know.

                    ROGER
        How are things with you?

                    DAEMON
        Things haven't changed with me for years.

                    ROGER
        Pretty ugly situation we've got with…uh…China,
        don't you think?

                    DAEMON
        You don't look so good either.

                    ROGER
        I? Oh, I'm fine. Fine. Just thought I'd drop
        around and tell you things were fine.

Daemon studies him a moment. Then he opens a drawer and pulls out the glove cleaner. He sets it on the table.

54.   CLOSE SHOT GLOVE CLEANER
       PULL BACK FOR TWO SHOT.

                    DAEMON
        I'm glad to hear it.

                    ROGER
                (silly laugh)
        Oh yes…the, ah…glove cleaner. Say, tell me
        something. Do you sell much of that?

                    DAEMON
        Now and again.

                    ROGER
        By the way, what's in it?

                    DAEMON
                (matter of fact)
        No trace, no odor, no taste, no way to detect its
        presence. And it's sure. One thousand dollars.

That's what you came for, isn't it?

                ROGER
Me? Why no…not at all.
       (pause)
Painless?

              DAEMON
Of course. It's perfect for its purpose. The only thing of its kind in the world.

                ROGER
Interesting.

              DAEMON
She loves you as I said she would, doesn't she? A constant love, and nothing you can do to her would change it. She worships and adores you, and hangs on your every word.

                ROGER
Oh yes…yes, she does.

              DAEMON
One thousand dollars.

                ROGER
    (breaking)
Look, Professor Daemon, I'm going out of my ever-lovin' mind. I can't stand it anymore!

              DAEMON
Naturally.

                ROGER
Is there such a thing as being loved too much? Isn't there some way to quiet down just a little?

              DAEMON
No.

ROGER
Isn't there a potion that would transfer some of this love to…someone else perhaps? Like a nice Cocker Spaniel maybe?

DAEMON
Not a chance. She's yours.

ROGER
She's so good to me, she's so very nice…

DAEMON
I know. The Glove Cleaner is the only way.

ROGER
I can't do that.

Daemon starts to put the bottle away.

ROGER
There must be another way.

Daemon brings out the bottle again.

DAEMON
This is the way. The only way. One thousand dollars.

ROGER
Doctor, you don't know what it's like. All the time, love-love-love!

DAEMON
I do know what it's like. How do you think I came to invent the Glove Cleaner?

ROGER
(sighs)
That's all my savings.

DAEMON
I know. It's always like that.

Roger writes a check and hands it to the doctor. Then he picks up the bottle and looks at it. He sighs.

> DAEMON
> No trace, no odor, no taste, no way to detect…

> ROGER
> (straining)
> All right.

> DAEMON
> One thing I must warn you about. You must use it immediately, do you hear me? Immediately, and you must use it all.

> ROGER
> Immediately? Why does it spoil?

> DAEMON
> No, but you will. Once you delay, you are lost, believe me. If you fail the first time you try to use it, you'll never have the courage to try again. Never.

> ROGER
> Goodbye, Professor Daemon.

> DAEMON
> Goodbye. It's always the same way—first the stimulant, then the chaser.

Roger nods and goes, taking the bottle.

DISSOLVE TO:

55. INT LEILA'S APARTMENT
     NIGHT   MED CLOSE SHOT   LEILA

Who is waiting at the window. Suddenly she looks, waves, throws a kiss.

56. FULL SHOT THE ROOM

As she runs to the mirror, arranges her hair then goes to the door. Roger enters with a split of champagne as in Act One.

> ROGER
> Party. Thought we ought to have a party. It isn't everybody who's been married six months like this.

He holds up the champagne.

> LEILA
> Oh, darling, what a lovely surprise. You told me you'd be late, and here you are with champagne.

> ROGER
> Glasses. Can't have a party without glasses.

He takes off is coat and goes to the bar table.

> LEILA
> It's just like the other time with a bottle, only this time you don't have to beg to stay.

She tries to kiss him and he endures it, then peels her off.

> ROGER
> Later. You sit down and let me bring it to you.
> (gestures)
> Over there…

> LEILA
> All right. Oh, do you want candlelight? It's so romantic. Let's have candlelight.

> ROGER
> (hurriedly)
> Sure, sure, sure, candlelight, shmandlelight, anything!

He is pulling the cork on the champagne. She gets candles and lights them as he pours.

57.   CLOSE SHOT ROGER'S HAND

As he takes the Glove Cleaner from his pocket, removes the stopper. He tilts the bottle ready to pour then stops. His hands tremble. He tries to pour again, but obviously can't.

> LEILA
> (during this)
> It's so wonderful being married to you, darling.
> I've never felt so completely happy in my life.
> I've lived to love you. Only you.

> ROGER
> (preoccupied with bottle)
> That's very nice...

> LEILA
> How did you happen to think of the champagne?

> ROGER
> It just came to me.

> LEILA
> I remember how you looked the first time you brought me champagne. Your eyes were filled with love, and you watched me drink...so sadly, because you thought it was to be our last drink. Remember?

> ROGER
> I remember.

He looks down at the Glove Cleaner that he has palmed in his hand.

> LEILA
> Baby bunny?
> (she nuzzles the back of his neck)
> Sweet little rabbit. I've got nooos for you!

58.   CLOSE SHOT ROGER

As his face turns white and he openly pours the bottle of cleaner into the glass, starts to turn to hand it to her when she gives him a bear hug. The glass slips out of his hand.

59.   CLOSE SHOT THE GLASS

As it smashes on the floor.

60.   CLOSE SHOT LEILA

> LEILA
> Oh my sweetest—I'm such a clumsy oaf—how can you love such a clumsy oaf? Here, my heart—take *my* glass.

She thrusts it on him. His eyes go down slowly to stare down at the floor.

> ROGER
> (very softly)
> It's all right. I couldn't have gone through with it. I could never have gone through with it.

Leila runs over to the couch, sits down, pats the pillow next to her.

> LEILA
> Lover marshmallow—come sit next to your Leila.

Like a man in a trance, he walks over and sits down next to her. She leans against him.

> LEILA
> Think of it. We'll spend the rest of our lives like this, won't we?

He nods, closes his eyes.

> ROGER
> The rest of our lives.

She nuzzles him, pinches him, nips at his ear, kisses him and is all over him. The CAMERA STARTS TO MOVE away until once again it is shooting down toward the street below. There stands Professor Daemon.

61.   ZOOM INTO EXTREMELY TIGHT CLOSE SHOT HIS FACE

As first he chuckles softly and then breaks out laughing a loud, raucous, terribly cruel laugh. The CAMERA STARTS TO MOVE up and away from him. The laugh persists for a long moment.

> NARRATOR'S VOICE
> Mr. Roger Shackleforth, who has discovered at this late date that love can be as sticky as a vat of molasses, as unpalatable as a hunk of spoiled yeast, and as all-consuming as a six-alarm fire in a bamboo and canvas tent. Case history of a lover-boy who should never have entered…
> The Twilight Zone!

FADE TO BLACK

<u>THE END</u>

WILLIAM IDELSON
"Long Distance Call"

William Idelson began his career in Hollywood as a radio and television actor. One of his earliest TV roles was in the first season *Twilight Zone* episode "A World of Difference" alongside Howard Duff, playing an assistant director on a fictional movie set. Idelson then turned to writing for television and went on to become one of the leading comedy writers of the 1960s and 70s, writing and co-writing scores of episodes for such shows as *The Andy Griffith Show, The Dick Van Dyke Show, The Odd Couple, Get Smart,* and *The Bob Newhart Show.* He also acted in bit parts on many of these TV shows.

"Long Distance Call" remains one of *The Twilight Zone*'s finest horror installments. Like Jerry Sohl's "Living Doll" and "Queen of the Nile," Serling's "To Serve Man," Matheson's "Nightmare at 20,000 Feet" and "Night Call," it has all the ingredients of a bonafide spine-chiller.

Idelson constructed the script with input from colleague-friend Charles Beaumont. The final version is credited to both writers, but the first draft of the script, titled "Direct Line," was written entirely by Idelson.

The television episode was one of six that Cayuga Productions shot on videotape. Use of tape was the result of CBS's attempt to save money. James Sheldon, who directed two of the six episodes, says, "The question I get most often about *The Twilight Zone* these days is why some of the episodes were shot on videotape. They wanted to try out these facilities at CBS Television City. But the possibilities were way too limited for a series like *The Twilight Zone*. A lot was lost without George T. Clemens [principal Director of Photography of the series]." The tape shows had no director of photography.

An interesting aspect of the family set-up of "Long Distance Call" is the possessiveness of the grandparent over the grandchild, and an icy, undemonstrative relationship between the in-laws. It's clear from the beginning that Billy Bayles' grandmother (on the father's side) and mother have a somewhat strained relationship, insofar as the grandmother believes that her grown-and-married son was taken away from her and that her grandchild is a replacement of her own "lost" child.

Hungarian-born actress Lili Darvas is splendid as the old and infirm grandmother. She is a villain of the truest form, but shows some mercy in the end and lets her grandson live. Philip Abbott and Patricia Smith submit sensitive performances as the parents.

In the lead as Billy Bayles (called "Paulie" in the first draft of the script) was Bill Mumy. Like Ron Howard and several other child actors working regularly during the same period, Mumy was already a fine performer by the age of five or six. Here, he displays a thoughtful intelligence and understanding of the part, versus a recitation of rote-memorized words. Pleased with Mumy's interpretation, James Sheldon cast him again a year later when assigned to direct the cult-favorite episode "It's a Good Life," where he played a vile little boy with the capability of obliterating anyone and anything that displeases him. Sheldon recalls, "Late one day during the shoot, I wanted to get one last shot of Billy before wrapping and going home. Child labor laws were, and still are, so strict—but his mother was a nice lady and agreed to let him do it. The next day, the studio found out about it…had the Child Labor people found out, I'd have really been in trouble! Needless to say, I never did that again." What Sheldon describes may be a shot that was one not included in the final print of the episode, with Mumy drowning in the patio pool. Had it been included, it surely would have made for a more terrifying climax. Associate Producer Del Reisman relates, "CBS was likely concerned that a child involved in such a scheme would've been perhaps a bit too suggestive. You never know what kids might try to do on their own!"

Two major scenes in the script were altered—the grandmother's hospital death scene was moved to the family home, and her funeral sequence was altogether omitted. But the most significant change was that of Chris Bayles' plea to his mother, delivered via the toy telephone, to let Billy live. This was a good choice. The original, which appears in the script printed in this volume, does not have the substance of the poignant final version. Bill Mumy recalls, "[The speech] was not working, and I remember that we actually stopped production for a couple hours while they re-wrote it. Philip Abbott played it very well. People still ask me about that episode."

"Long Distance Call" was originally broadcast on 31 March, 1961.

LONG DISTANCE CALL

CAST

CHRIS BAYLES	Moderately attractive man in his early thirties, sensitive, intelligent. Not in the least a momma's boy, despite his love for
GRANDMA BAYLES	Chris' mother. Born in an unspecified 'old country' she has never completely 'Americanized' herself. Seventy-five-years old, Grandma is a woman of small intelligence and powerful emotions; wholly without guile, a simple, almost animalistic creature falling rapidly into senility. Her existence is ruled by love and loneliness.
SYLVIA BAYLES	Quick, perceptive woman of twenty-nine or thirty, a dramatic contrast to Grandma.
BILLY BAYLES	A bright four-year-old, given to moodiness and an almost mystical communion with his grandmother.
SHIRLEY	The baby sitter, a plump, not terribly sharp fifteen-year-old.
MR. PETERSON	A businessman in his fifties.
DR. UNGER	Distinguished, gray-thatched family physician, on first name terms with the Bayleses.

ATTENDANT
MINISTER
FUNERAL DIRECTOR

SETS

Bayles living room, patio, child's bedroom, parents' bedroom, hospital room, funeral parlor

FORMAT INTRODUCTION
FADE IN:

INT. BAYLES HOUSE – DINING ROOM – DAY
CLOSE – ON CAKE

A round, fluffy birthday cake, with four pink penny candles thrusting up crookedly from the frosting. A woman's hand reaches INTO FRAME with a match. The candles are lit, one by one, as CAMERA PULLS BACK for FULL SHOT. In the small traditional dining room we see CHRIS BAYLES, his wife, SYLVIA, and his mother, GRANDMA BAYLES, all of whom are singing the HAPPY BIRTHDAY song to Chris' young son, BILLY.

>   CHRIS, SYLVIA, GRANDMA
>   (more or less in unison)
>   Happy birthday to you,
>   Happy birthday to you,
>   Happy birthday to Billy,
>   Happy birthday to you!

Billy is as delighted as any healthy four-year-old: he grins all over his face and joins the others in applause.

>   GRANDMA
>   (with accent)
>   Wait, now, boy, wait. You got to blow out the
>   candles or it is no good.

>   BILLY
>   (bending forward)
>   Can't reach 'em.

>   GRANDMA
>   Well…

She gets up, turns off the lights, then walks to Billy's chair and lifts the boy over the table.

CLOSE TWO SHOT - GRANDMA AND BILLY

The flickering candles splash eerie light over the old woman and the child.

CLOSE SHOT – CHRIS

      CHRIS
 Ma...

BILLY FAVORING GRANDMA AND

Grandma lifting the boy.

      GRANDMA
    (demanding silence)
 Shuh...shuh...shuh.

      CHRIS
 Ma, you know what the doctor said about
 exerting yourself.

Grandma will have none of it. Ignoring her son, she hefts Billy to within inches of the cake.

      GRANDMA
 Take a big breath, Billy, and *blow them out!*
 All of them!

Billy does so. Laughing, but obviously affected by her labors, Grandma sets the child back in his high chair.

      GRANDMA
    (to Billy)
 You make a wish?

He nods grinning.

      GRANDMA (Cont'd)
 What it was? You tell Grandma.

She puts her ear next to Billy's mouth and smiles and nods as he whispers.

      SYLVIA
 Don't you think we might all hear the wish, Billy?

> GRANDMA
> Is a secret, between him and me. Ain't that so?

Billy nods, a willing conspirator. Breathing heavily, Grandma begins to cut the cake.

> CHRIS
> Ma, why don't you let Syl do that?

> GRANDMA
> (smiling)
> What you think, I am too old to lift a knife?
> When I am that old, you get a shovel and dig the hole.

> BILLY
> Shovel!

> GRANDMA
> Yes, my angel!
> (gives the cake to Billy)
> Oh, my heart is so full, I…like to say something. Could I say something?

> CHRIS
> Sure.

Grandma stands, her eyes alight, almost trembling with the love that suffuses her. She looks at her grandson as she speaks. The words are really for him alone.

> GRANDMA
> (softly)
> My little, Billy…my wonderful little boy.
> He gave me life again. An old woman, good for nothing no more but to complain…he held out his hands to me, and made me alive.

Grandma begins to cry, suddenly and for no apparent reason, the way very old people do.

> BILLY
> Why you crying, Grandma?

GRANDMA
(pathetically)
I don't know, angel. Maybe it is because I won't be here with you for very long.

BILLY
Why not?

GRANDMA
I will be away.

BILLY
Where?

CHRIS
Nowhere. Grandma's going to be right here, Billy, next year and the year after that—

GRANDMA
No, don't lie to him!
(with finality)
I will be gone.

Billy rushes into Grandma's arms, and she holds high tight and cries over him. Sylvia and Chris exchange a disturbed look.

CHRIS
Hey, time for presents!

Chris gets up and turns on the lights. This breaks the spell for Billy. He rushes over to his father and accompanies him toward the living room, o.s. Sylvia remains.

SYLVIA
(looking at Grandma)
Is anything wrong, Gran?

GRANDMA
(rising proudly)
No. A little short of breath . . . You go on.

Sylvia walks off to join Chris and Billy. Grandma gets up from the chair with difficulty, shuffles over to a bureau, opens it, withdraws a square package, and starts for the living room.

INT. LIVING ROOM - FULL SHOT

Billy is ripping packages apart as fast as he can. The floor is littered with fancy paper and ribbons, and strewn about are: A MINIATURE BASEBALL BAT, A PAIR OF BOXING GLOVES, A SET OF CRAYONS, and A PLASTIC ROCKET LAUNCHER. At the moment, Billy is unwrapping a rather formidable toy PISTOL.

                      BILLY
               (pretending to shoot)
   Bang! *Bang!*

Grandma ENTERS.

                    GRANDMA
   Billy?

Billy stops. He and his parents look up at Grandma.

                GRANDMA (Cont'd)
          (holding out the package)
   Don't you want to see what Grandma got you?

Billy drops the gun, dashes over to Grandma, snatches away the package and tears it open. From the cardboard box, he removes a toy version of an old-fashioned wall telephone.

CLOSE ON TELEPHONE

                  BILLY (o.s)
   Telephone!

BACK TO SCENE

She makes an imaginary phone with one fist at her mouth, another at her ear.

                GRANDMA Cont'd)
   Hello! Hello! Is there somebody calling Grandma?

                    BILLY
            (into toy phone; delighted)
        It's me, Billy!

They all laugh. Grandma takes a few steps toward Billy, then stops. She winces with pain and puts a hand to her heart.

                    CHRIS
        Ma? You all right?

Another step. A look of fear and confusion. She gives a little gasp and staggers. Chris rushes up and helps her to the couch. She is breathing raggedly.

                    CHRIS
            (to Sylvia)
        Call Doctor Unger, quick!

Billy is, of course, terrified. He begins to cry.

                    BILLY
        What's the matter with Gramma?

                    CHRIS
            (holding Grandma's head in his arms)
        Nothing…she's sick, that's all.

                    BILLY
        I want to talk with her.

                    CHRIS
        You can't. Get away!

Billy retreats. CAMERA FOLLOWS as he sits down on the floor, near to the telephone. Impulsively he picks it up and puts the receiver to his ear.

                    BILLY
        Gramma…
            (into toy phone)
        …don't be sick. Don't be sick, Gramma…
        This is Billy. Don't be sick…

CAMERA WHIP PANS to SERLING, who is standing in another part of the room.

> SERLING
> Everyone knows what a telephone is, and what it does...but how many of us know *why*? When we pick up that familiar object and talk to people we've never seen...and listen to their voices come flying back to us across thousands of miles...how many of us give it a second thought?
> (beat)
> Not many. But we might, if...like Billy Bayles ...we found ourselves connected with The Twilight Zone...

FADE TO BLACK

FADE IN:

INT. HOSPITAL WAITING ROOM - MED. SHOT - NIGHT

Church-silent, oppressive with the murk of suffering. Chris is standing by a window, staring into the blackness; Sylvia and Billy are on the couch by the wall.

> BILLY
> I want to see Gramma.

> SYLVIA
> (softly)
> Soon, darling.

Billy is restive. Not comprehending the situation, he twists and turns impatiently.

DOCTOR UNGER ENTERS. He is a tall, graying man in his late fifties. Chris walks over to him.

> DOCTOR UNGER
> (after a beat)
> I'm afraid there's nothing we can do, Chris.

> CHRIS
> Is she...

                    DOCTOR UNGER
    Not yet. She could last the night, or...
            (he shrugs)
    She isn't in any pain.

                    CHRIS
    Can we see her?

                    DOCTOR UNGER
    I wouldn't advise it. Not that it would hurt her,
    but — well, I doubt that she'd recognize you.

                    CHRIS
    I'd recognize her.

                    DOCTOR UNGER
    All right, Chris.

Shaken by the experience to come, Chris rather foolishly straightens his tie and runs a hand through his hair.

                    CHRIS
            (to Sylvia)
    You might as well go home.

                    BILLY
    I want to see Gramma.

                    CHRIS
    Billy...Grandma's sick, you understand?
    Very sick. Why don't you wait until she's well...

                    BILLY
            (beginning to cry)
    I want to see her now!

                    SYLVIA
    Billy, stop that.

But the child can't stop. His voice rises in pitiful little cries.

                              CHRIS
                    (glancing at the doctor)
               All right. But only for a couple of minutes.
               And, Billy, if Grandma acts a little…strange…
               that's only because of the medicine.
                         (hands him a handkerchief)
               Now blow.

They all follow the doctor out of the waiting room, into the corridor.

INT. HOSPITAL CORRIDOR - AT THE DOOR TO GRANDMA'S ROOM

Doctor Unger walks into scene, opens the door and gestures quietly to Chris. Taking a breath, Chris ENTERS, followed by Sylvia and Billy.

INT. HOSPITAL ROOM - FAVORING GRANDMA

Without the assistance of cosmetics and street clothes, she looks very old indeed, far older than her seventy-five years. A hospital attendant has combed her hair out onto the pillow in a soft silver wave. Now Grandma's eyes are open, staring up blindly at the ceiling. She is waiting for death.

Chris looks at Sylvia, then at Doctor Unger — whose answering look says: "You see, she's beyond us all now." Then, out of the stillness, Billy breaks into a little cry and runs to the bed before anyone can stop him.

                              BILLY
               Grandma!

Slowly Grandma's head turns. The blankness goes from her eyes. Her desiccated hand lifts and touches Billy's hair.

                            GRANDMA
                       (almost inaudibly)
               Hello, my angel…

                              BILLY
               Are you sick, Gramma?

                            GRANDMA
               Not no more.

BILLY
Then why don't you come home with us?

CHRIS
Hello, ma.

Chris and Sylvia move toward the bed. Grandma looks up at them as if they were total strangers.

GRANDMA
(to Chris)
Who are you?

CHRIS
Chris...your son.

GRANDMA
(very feebly)
No...no...my son was taken from me...
by a woman...
(pointing at Sylvia)
...that woman...
(touching Billy again)
...this is my son now...Billy, my son...

She closes her eyes a moment. A tear rolls down her face.

BILLY
What's the matter, Gramma.

GRANDMA
I am thinking...how lonely it will be. Oh, Billy, I wish you could go with Grandma...

BILLY
Where?

GRANDMA
(weakening fast)
Away...far away...together, the two of us, Billy...
just you and me...just you and me, Billy...no one else...just you...and me.

She gasps once and is still. There is death in her wide-open eyes. Billy stares at her, not understanding.

>   BILLY
>   Grandma? Grandma!

>   CHRIS
>   Son, I think —

>   BILLY
>   (suddenly terrified; a shrill scream)
>   *Grandma!*

DISSOLVE TO:

EXT. BAYLES BACKYARD - HIGH ANGLE DOWN ON FISH POND

Showing the fish, darting like slivers of gold beneath the smooth green surface of the water. We see the REFLECTION of Billy standing above the pond, staring into its depths.

>   SYLVIA (o.s.)
>   Billy!

Billy does not move. Presently we see the reflection of Sylvia.

MED. SHOT - BY THE POND

This pond is one of the cheap department store models: a shallow rubber mold, an assortment of rocks and plastic lilies. Sylvia snatches Billy away.

>   SYLVIA
>   Billy, didn't you hear me calling you?

>   BILLY
>   (almost as though dazed)
>   No.

>   SYLVIA
>   You know you're not supposed to be playing
>   around the pond.

He doesn't answer.

                    SYLVIA (Cont'd)
              What were you doing?

                        BILLY
              Looking at the fishes.

                       SYLVIA
                   (after a beat)
              I think you'd better come in now. It's getting cold.

They walk away from the pond.

INT. BAYLES HOUSE – LIVING ROOM – MED. SHOT

Sylvia and Billy ENTER. Chris is in an easy chair, smoking a pipe.

                       SYLVIA
                    (to Billy)
              You go on into the playroom.

Billy obeys. Totally without exuberance, he turns and walks to the o.s. playroom. Sylvia watches him.

                        CHRIS
              What's the matter?

                       SYLVIA
              Billy. He's been walking around in a trance
              all day.

                        CHRIS
              Well, after last night…it must have hit him pretty
              hard. You know how close they were.

                       SYLVIA
                   (nodding; almost to herself)
              Yes. I know

                        CHRIS
                   (taking offense at her tone)
              What do you mean by that?

                    SYLVIA
          (defensively)
     I mean they were too close. It wasn't right.
     And you know it.

                    CHRIS
     Honey...

                    SYLVIA
     You heard what she said at the hospital!

                    CHRIS
     She didn't mean it.

                    SYLVIA
     Didn't she?

                    CHRIS
          (angrily)
     No! For heaven's sake, Sylvia—she was full of
     sedatives...and she was dying.

Sylvia realizes how badly she's behaving. Remorseful, she goes to Chris.

                    SYLVIA
     I'm sorry, darling. It's just that...I guess we're
     all upset.

Suddenly Sylvia falls silent. She listens to a tiny SOUND o.s. It is Billy's voice.

                    BILLY (o.s.)
          (happily)
     Hey, Grandma...why don't you come and play?
          (pause)
     Is it cold there?
          (pause; he giggles happily)
     I had weenies for lunch! What'd you have?

Sylvia looks at Chris, then turns and walks toward the playroom. CAMERA MOVES WITH HER.

AT PLAYROOM

Louvered French doors are closed. Through them we hear:

> BILLY (o.s)
> Mommie caught me...I couldn't...
> (again he laughs)

Sylvia opens one of the doors, quickly.

INT. PLAYROOM - MED. SHOT

Billy is sitting in a corner, near a stack of playthings. The toy telephone is in front of him. He looks up (TOWARD CAMERA) and puts the receiver slowly down on its hook. Sylvia ENTERS SHOT.

> SYLVIA
> Who were you talking to, Billy.

> BILLY
> (very matter of fact)
> Gramma.

CAMERA MOVES IN for CLOSE SHOT of Billy and telephone.

> BILLY (Cont'd)
> She says she's lonesome. She wants me to come
> and stay with her. Can I, Momma? Can I?

FADE TO BLACK:

FADE IN:

INT. FUNERAL PARLOR - FAVORING MINISTER - DAY

A hawk-faced solemn man is intoning obsequies for Grandma Bayles, who lies in her coffin surrounded by wreaths. We do not yet see her.

> MINISTER
> The Lord giveth and the Lord taketh away. Blessed
> by the name of the Lord. We are here to say
> farewell to the earthly remains of Sarah Bayles,
> a devoted wife, mother and grandmother...

MED. SHOT - FUNERAL PARLOR

The event of Grandma Bayles' leave-taking has attracted few mourners. Apart from Chris and Sylvia, there are only the half-dozen faceless ones who seem to be present at every funeral. The minister's voice drones on in the b.g., an indistinguishable murmur in the dim silence. Chris and Sylvia are seated in flimsy metal fold-up chairs.

TWO SHOT - CHRIS AND SYLVIA

       CHRIS
     (whispering)
   I could do without that.

Sylvia gives him a look.

      CHRIS (Cont'd)
   So could she. Ma never liked a fuss.

Suddenly Chris' calm collapses. Unwilling tears spring to his eyes, and he makes hard fists.

       SYLVIA
   I'm sorry, Chris.

She touches his arm, and this seems to help. In the b.g. now we hear THE ROCK OF AGES being played on a whiney electric organ. We can almost smell the sickly sweet odor of the flowers. The Funeral Director walks up, all sorrow and commiseration.

      FUNERAL DIRECTOR
   You may see your mother now.

Chris looks up, bring his thoughts back to the time and the place, and rises. He and Sylvia follow the man in the direction of the casket.

ANGLE ON CASKET

As Chris and Sylvia walk up, the CAMERA MOVES UP to INCLUDE GRANDMA, who lies upon the white silk froth like a figure carved of candle wax. Her eyes are closed, but she does not look as if she's sleeping. She looks dead.

Chris pauses only a moment, then draws a breath and hurries on. Sylvia continues to stare at the remains of her one-time antagonist, and there is a trace of pity — if not regret — in her face. Then she, too, hurries OUT OF SCENE.

CAMERA MOVES IN SLOWLY for EXTREME CLOSE SHOT of Grandma. If her eyes were to open now, we would all surely die of fright. But of course her eyes do not open. They will never open. As CAMERA IS UPON THE DEAD FACE, we,

DISSOLVE TO:

INT. BAYLES HOUSE - LIVING ROOM - MED. SHOT

Chris and Sylvia ENTER. Chris takes off his coat, slowly, still numb with grief.

> SYLVIA
> You want to be alone?

> CHRIS
> No. That's the last thing I want.

> SYLVIA
> Okay. I'll make us some coffee.

She turns and starts for the kitchen just as SHIRLEY the babysitter, comes into the room. Shirley, a plump fifteen-year-old, is obviously quite upset.

> SHIRLEY
> Mrs. Bayles!

> SYLVIA
> Yes?
> (suddenly fearful)
> What is it, Shirley.

A MAN walks out of the dining room area. He is middle-aged, dressed in a sober gray suit. The sight of him freezes Sylvia.

> PETERSON
> Mrs. Bayles, my name is Peterson. I'm sorry to bother you at a time like this...the girl told me about your unhappiness...but—

SYLVIA
What is it?

Chris joins the group.

PETERSON
Well, it's about your boy.

SYLVIA
Billy?!
    (on the edge of hysteria)

SHIRLEY
He's all right, Mrs. Bayles. I put him to sleep an hour ago.

CHRIS
What about Billy, Mr. Peterson?

PETERSON
Mr. Bayles?
    (Chris nods)
Well, now, I sure hate to say this…but your son almost got himself killed a while ago. Ran right out in front of my car. From nowhere! Lucky thing I'm a cautious driver, Mr. Bayles. If I wasn't, you'd have had two funerals on your hands today.

Sylvia turns and runs toward the stairs, o.s.

CHRIS
Billy never plays on the streets.

SHIRLEY
I *know*. That why I didn't say anything when he went out.

CHRIS
What happened?

PETERSON
Well, there wasn't any sense in putting on the

brakes—he was too close—so I cut the wheel as sharp as I could. I couldn't have missed him by more than a few inches.

SHIRLEY
It wasn't my fault, Mr. Bayles. Honest.

CHRIS
All right, Shirley. Apparently it wasn't anyone's fault.

PETERSON
I'll call the police, if you want me to.

CHRIS
No, I don't see what that would accomplish. Thank you, Mr. Peterson.

PETERSON
Mr. Bayles...this isn't any of my business, but...
I got a couple of kids myself...and I know how much they mean...how precious they are...
(has difficulty phrasing it)
I think you'd better have a talk with your boy.

Sylvia re-enters the room, having assured herself of Billy's safety. She listens.

CHRIS
A talk? Why?

PETERSON
Well...when I saw that he was all right, I asked him, why did he do a crazy thing like that, running out in the middle of a busy street...
(beat)
He said somebody told him to.

SYLVIA
Who?

PETERSON
(turning to face her)
He didn't say, ma'am.

SHIRLEY
(genuinely upset)
You know I wouldn't tell Billy to do anything like that.

SYLVIA
Who else did he talk to, Shirley?

SHIRLEY
No one. He didn't talk to no one. All day long, he just sat in the playroom playing with that toy telephone ...*Honest*!

Chris looks at Sylvia, whose thoughts are plainly written on her face.

SYLVIA
Come upstairs, Chris.

CHRIS
All right. I'll be there in a minute.

CAMERA FOLLOWS SYLVIA as she walks to the stairs. In b.g. we HEAR:

CHRIS
I'm sorry, Mr. Peterson.

PETERSON
Don't be sorry. Be glad. The boy's safe.

Sylvia is in f.g. She listens another moment, then starts up the stairs.

CUT TO:

INT. BAYLES HOUSE - UPSTAIRS HALLWAY AT BILLY'S DOOR

Sylvia listens, her ear at the door. From inside the room we hear CHILDISH GIGGLING and an incomprehensible monologue. Chris walks INTO SCENE. Sylvia gestures for silence.

SYLVIA
Listen.

Chris looks at his wife, hesitantly places his ear near the door, then says:

> CHRIS
> Oh, for heavens sake!

He opens the door.

INT. BILLY'S ROOM - MED. SHOT

The boy's laughter ceases abruptly. He is facing away from his parents.

> CHRIS
> Hey Punkin'—we're back.

Slowly, Billy turns and faces Chris and Sylvia. His face is as void of expression as Grandma's had been. He places the telephone receiver back into its cradle.

> CHRIS (Cont'd)
> What's this running in the street business?
> (bends down and lifts the boy into his arms)
> Billy?
> (passes his hands before the child's eyes, half-humorously)
> You know, you worried us.

> BILLY
> (expressionless)
> I'm sorry, Daddy.

> CHRIS
> Why'd you do it?

> BILLY
> (evasively)
> I don't know.

> SYLVIA
> Billy, who were you talking to on the phone just now?

BILLY
(looking away)
Nobody.

SYLVIA
Billy...don't fib to me. Who were you talking to?

BILLY
(beginning to cry)
Nobody! Nobody!

Sylvia takes Billy's shoulders roughly and shakes the boy.

SYLVIA
(losing control)
You're going to tell me! You hear?

CHRIS
Sylvia! Get ahold of yourself!

Sylvia turns and runs from the room.

BILLY
Mommie doesn't like Grandma, does she?

CHRIS
Of course she does. She's just upset.
(puts Billy down and starts for the door)
Billy...I've got to tell you something. Try to understand. You won't be seeing Grandma anymore. She didn't go away, like we said...she died, Billy. Do you know what that means?

BILLY
Yes.

CHRIS
Now I know you're only pretending to talk to her on the telephone...I know it's a game you made up...but, please, Billy, for me...don't do it around Mommy.

                        BILLY
Why?

                        CHRIS
Because...well...just don't.

                        BILLY
All right, Daddy.

Chris looks again at his son, then EXITS THE ROOM.

EXT. BILLY'S ROOM - REVERSE

Chris steps out into the hallway, lights a cigarette and pretends for a moment that he is not listening. Exhaling a cloud of smoke, he walks away. CAMERA HOLDS on the closed door, and presently we HEAR again the SOUND of childish laughter, muted and conspiratorial.

                                        DISSOLVE TO:

INT. BAYLES HOUSE - MASTER BEDROOM - NIGHT

A small bedroom, with double bed, bureau, nightstand, tasteful prints. Chris is seated by the window. He is clad in pajamas and robe. All of his early life and good times and the forgotten moments, suddenly remembered, are in his eyes. Sylvia comes out of the bathroom.

                        SYLVIA
Darling, aren't you coming to bed?

He doesn't hear her. His mind is back in another house, in another time.

                        SYLVIA Cont'd)
                    (going to him)
Don't shut me out, Chris.

                        CHRIS
I'm sorry. I was just...

                        SYLVIA
I know.

CHRIS
(angrily)
Funerals stink. I wish we hadn't gone. Now I'll always think of her lying there like a... wax dummy...
(stubs his cigarette out)
Syl, I know how hard it was for you...what you went through...but she didn't mean you any harm.

SYLVIA
I suppose not.

CHRIS
(rises; starts to take off the robe)
It's true. She had four children before me, remember, and lost them and...well, she couldn't let go. I was all she had.

SYLVIA
Except for Billy.

CHRIS
Billy was me again...a chance to go back, to pretend that none of the years had happened...
(sighs)
Oh, it wasn't right...or fair to you...but honey, believe me—whatever she did, she did out of love.

SYLVIA
For whom?

Realizing how this must hurt Chris, she holds him close and says quickly:

SYLVIA (Cont'd)
I'm sorry. I didn't mean that. Really I didn't, Chris.

CHRIS
You're trembling.

SYLVIA
Let's go to bed.

They go to the bed and climb under the covers. Sylvia kisses Chris and turns out the light.

        SYLVIA (Cont'd)
    Good night, darling.

        CHRIS
 Good night.

As CAMERA MOVES in on Sylvia, there is a DISSOLVE EFFECT, showing a passage of time . . . perhaps an hour. the room is very quiet. We see a clock, reading three a.m. Suddenly Sylvia's eyes open, wide. She listens. We hear nothing but the TICKING of the clock. Sylvia waits a moment, stricken by fear; then she sits up, glances at Chris, who is sleeping, listens a moment more, then rises. Throwing on her dressing gown, she walks softly across the room.

HALLWAY - CLOSE ON BILLY'S DOOR - NIGHT

Nothing but quiet shadows in the hall. Sylvia walks to the door, hesitates an agonizing moment, then eases the door open.

INT. BILLY'S ROOM - ANGLE ON CRIB - SYLVIA'S POV

Sitting in a willow-soft patch of moonlight, Billy is babbling into the toy telephone. He doesn't notice his mother.

        BILLY
  Will you give me an ice cream bar? When?
   (pause; the child giggles madly)

Overcoming her fear, Sylvia tiptoes into the room. She bends over Billy, snatches the phone away from him and holds the receiver to her ear.

CLOSE UP - SYLVIA

Her face lit by the moonlight as she listens to the phone. Her eyes widen in horror.

        BILLY (o.s)
   My telephone! My telephone!

CUT TO:

INT. MASTER BEDROOM - MED. SHOT

Chris is awakened by Billy's cries. He jumps out of bed and runs across the room toward the door.

INT. BILLY'S ROOM - ON DOOR

Chris bursts in. CAMERA FOLLOWS HIM to Billy's bed. Billy is shrieking. Sylvia is staring at the phone, which lies on the floor.

> CHRIS
> Syl — what's wrong? What's the matter.

> SYLVIA
> I heard her.

> CHRIS
> Heard who? *Syl!*

> SYLVIA
> (babbling)
> She was there! On the phone…she didn't say anything…but I could hear her *breathing*… Oh, Chris…

Chris is frightened by her. He takes her by the shoulders.

> CHRIS
> Come on, honey…snap out of it.

She shakes him off. She is now like a person possessed.

> SYLVIA
> Let go of me! Billy! Is Billy all right?

> CHRIS
> Yes. Of course he is…

Chris turns and, CAMERA FOLLOWING, looks at the crib. It is empty. Chris stares, blinks. Sylvia, seeing her husband's face, leaps up with a cry. For an instant they look at they empty crib, then Sylvia rushes from the room.

> SYLVIA
> Billy!

> CHRIS
> Where are you going?

Quickly, he follows her.

EXT. BAYLES HOUSE - ON BACK DOOR - NIGHT

It is very dark. The door opens and Sylvia runs out, into f.g. What she sees stops her. Her fist goes to her mouth. Chris appears, looks in the direction of the fish pond, and runs, out of frame, toward it. CAMERA HOLDS on Sylvia.

> SYLVIA
> Oh, no...no...no...no...no...no...

DISSOLVE TO:

INT. BAYLES HOUSE - LIVING ROOM - MED. SHOT

Chris holds Sylvia, who is on the verge of collapse. O.s. we HEAR the rhythmic SOUND of the RESUSCITATOR PUMP.

> CHRIS
> Take it easy, honey...please. He's going to be all right.

> SYLVIA
> She took him away...she took him...

Chris can't stand to hear her say this. He clutches her tightly, as though to shake these thoughts out of her.

> CHRIS
> Syl! Don't say that!

                    SYLVIA
                  (monotone)
              She took him away.

Chris gets up and walks to the other side of the room. Sylvia stares straight ahead, uncomprehending.

ANGLE ON CHRIS

Standing by the door to the dining room. He looks in, then turns away. We hear the resuscitator working relentlessly. An attendant walks out.

                    CHRIS
              How—how is it?

                   ATTENDANT
              (pained by what he must say)
          If we'd got him a few minutes earlier…

Chris closes his eyes, takes a trembling breath.

                ATTENDANT (Cont'd)
          The doctor'll be here in a minute. He'll give
          your wife something.

Chris nods. CAMERA FOLLOWS as he walks, blindly, away from the attendant. He looks at Sylvia, then back in the direction of the dining room. Then he turns and moves toward the hallway.

UPSTAIRS HALLWAY

Chris walks to Billy's room and ENTERS.

INT. BILLY'S ROOM - REVERSE

Chris hurries in, looks about for a moment, then fastens his eyes on:

CLOSE SHOT - THE TOY TELEPHONE

WIDER SHOT

Perspiring and panicky Chris goes to the phone and picks it up. After a split-second's hesitation, he lifts the receiver to his mouth. CAMERA MOVES IN as he speaks.

> CHRIS
> Ma! Ma, if you can hear me...give him back to us...You said you loved me, and I know you did...I remember so many things. Remember that funny little dog I had? You let me keep him even when he tore up all the furniture...Pa wanted to give him away, but you said no. And remember the first day of school? How scared I was...and you sat in the back of the room all morning so I wouldn't cry? And that first pair of long pants... and the time I broke the window with the ball? You hid me under the bed when the policeman came...My graduation...And that first date I had, you remember? With that skinny redhead...how mad you were? We had lots of fights...but I always knew you loved me. And I loved you, too...so very, very much...I never really got a chance to tell you...Oh, Ma, please...give him back to us, so we can love him, too...give him back to us...

Sobbing, Chris lowers the toy phone and finally it drops from his fingers to the floor. He stands very still for a long time.

INT. DINING ROOM - CLOSE ON RESUSICITATOR

Pumping its steady rhythm. CAMERA MOVES UP to FACES OF THE ATTENDANTS. One of them breaks into a wide grin.

> ATTENDANT
> Hey. Hey...I think we *got* him!
> (pause)
> Yeah!

He turns. CAMERA MOVES BACK to INCLUDE Chris, who has just entered.

> CHRIS
> Is he...

Sylvia walks to Chris and stands in an agony of expectancy.

       ATTENDANT
      (nodding)
    I don't know how it happened, but…he's gonna
    be okay.

Sylvia closes her eyes in silent joy and slumps against Chris. He holds her tightly. Tears of happiness roll down his face.

       SERLING'S VOICE
    A toy telephone…an act of faith…and a miracle,
    sent all the way from that misty region known as
    The Twilight Zone.

              FADE OUT.

THE END

E. JACK NEUMAN
"The Trouble With Templeton"

One of the finest yet least-touted segments of *The Twilight Zone* is "The Trouble With Templeton," beautifully written by Ernst Jack Neuman (1921-1998). Rod Serling had written a similar *Zone* story earlier, "The Sixteen Millimeter Shrine," in which an aging Hollywood diva goes back to the era that she so longs to be a part of. Neuman went this several steps better, creating an even more expansive, and moving, fantasy. Booth Templeton, star of numerous Broadway plays—of late on an emotional decline, travels through time and gains the stamina he needs to continue working.

Neuman today is recognized as a major contributor to television, having worked for almost every major Hollywood studio for four decades beginning in the mid-1950s. He wrote numerous episodes of classic television, many of which were pilot episodes for what later became critically-acclaimed TV series. He created and wrote the pilots for *Dr. Kildare, Sam Benedict, Mr. Novak* (for which he won a Peabody Award in 1964), *Shenandoah,* and *Police Story.* Neuman also wrote the first mini-series ever produced on TV, *The Blue Knight*, which later became a full-fledged series. His film credits include the screenplays for "The Singing Nun" (co-written with alumnus *Twilight Zone* writer John Furia), "Heat Wave," "The Most Dangerous Game," "The Venetian Affair," and "Company of Killers." Neuman's formal training began at the University of Missouri journalism school, but was interrupted by World War II. He wrote his first screenplay, "The Silver Bandit," for King Brothers Productions in 1945 while hospitalized for a year at the US Naval Hospital in San Diego, recovering from tuberculosis. Soon after, he began writing dramas for radio. A high point in Neuman's career came in 1981 with the Emmy-nominated mini-series "Inside the Third Reich," based on the life of Hitler protègè Albert Speer.

He received four Writers Guild Awards, four Edgar Allan Poe Awards, plus some forty other honors. Neuman's personalized writing style was also evident in his writing for radio in the 1950s. Throughout his years of work in Hollywood, he taught writing at UCLA and University of Southern California, as well as pro-bono teaching at Terminal Island Prison in California.

"The Trouble With Templeton" (originally titled "The Strange Debut") holds true to *The Twilight Zone*'s ideals. Neuman had a remarkably vivid mental picture of how this story would play out, evidenced by detailed stage directions and descriptions of each character's persona. Templeton is an endearing soul, a throwback to a bygone era. Portrayed masterfully by Brian Aherne, he represents a highly old-school sophisticate. Aherne himself identified with much of what he was called upon to do here. Associate Producer Del Reisman recalls, "Brian Aherne had done "Juarez" back in the late '30s with Paul Muni, in addition to many other films. He was a legendary actor but hadn't done a lot of television and he didn't work much after that. He was past his prime as well, and fit into the role perfectly...almost as if he *was* Booth Templeton."

Buzz Kulik guided a fine group of supporting actors including Pippa Scott in a bravura performance as Laura, Charles Carlson as Barney, King Calder as the play's loquacious underwriter and Dave Willock as Templeton's chauffeur. All balance Aherne's rock-of-Gibraltar presence. As an added bonus, the episode was inexpensive to produce. The backlots and soundstages of MGM Studios were utilized for the street scenes. The director of Templeton's play was—fittingly enough—portrayed by none other than one of the greatest directors of our time, Sydney Pollack, who offers a remarkably humorous reading of a no-nonsense dictator of his charges. The script hails him as a genius, but it's apparent that *this* young lad is most likely no more than a Broadway flyweight.

One of the most poignant scenes in all of *The Twilight Zone*, and surely all of television, comes when Templeton picks up a music box, activates it, and begins to talk of his long-dead wife, Laura, to his devoted houseboy. "Eighteen when we were married, Marty...twenty-five when she died. Why did He have to take her away from me?" An equally spellbinding minute or so comes in the climax of the second act when Templeton storms out of the speakeasy after reuniting with Laura. The music stops, with all eyes on him exiting. There is a long shot of her. The lights go black as their ephemeral world vanishes and he returns to the present.

Neuman wisely avoided what could've been written as a predictably subtle transition between the past and present by placing an unexpected punchline in the middle of the story instead of the usual *Twilight Zone* twist at the end. Templeton stumbles out of the rehearsal in a desperate attempt to escape the present, only to find a crowd of applauding onlookers, and shortly thereafter realizes he's back in time.

The story has no surprise ending; it concludes triumphantly as the main character undergoes a progressive transformation to a renewed life, full of vitality.

The writer's work continues to make an impact. Neuman's wife Marian recalls, "I hadn't seen the episode in many, many years and not long ago I caught a rerun late one night. I didn't know it was Jack's episode—and I said to myself, 'Gee, whoever wrote this writes exactly like he did.' Then I saw the ending credits and lo and behold, there was his name."

John Furia, Jr. remembers Neuman with fondness. "Jack Neuman was an extraordinarily fine writer with a tough, passionate "voice" and a devotion to the integrity of his work. In person he had a rough edge but a most generous heart; a kind, thoughtful man. You could count on Jack to give you his honest opinion on any subject, including your latest script, while holding nothing back to spare your feelings. As a result many of us writer friends treasured his critiques because we knew we were getting "the straight Neuman" with no sugar coating. What he appreciated in your work, he praised with honesty and without hyperbole. Where he thought your imagination or inspiration flagged, he let you know clearly, forcefully, but also in most cases with a thoughtful suggestion or two about how you might improve it."

"The Trouble With Templeton" was originally broadcast on 12 December, 1960.

THE TROUBLE WITH TEMPLETON

<u>CAST</u>

BOOTH TEMPLETON	A handsome, successful actor in his late fifties
LAURA TEMPLETON	A sweet girl, suddenly turned brash
MARTY	Templeton's gentle and understanding valet and chauffeur. Long in Booth's service.
DORIS TEMPLETON	Thirtyish and inconsiderate.
ED PAGE	A play boy of thirty.
SIDNEY SPERRY	Lately come into the luxurious ability to finance a Broadway play.
ARTHUR WILLIS	A young genius of a director
EDDIE	A cheerful theatre doorman
FREDDIE	Restaurant owner and gangster-type of the 1920's
BARNEY FLUEGER	Tough, young, intellectual.

<u>SETS</u>

INT. Booth's Bedroom
INT. Theater Backstage
INT. Speakeasy and Hallway – Bandstand

EXT. House Side Yard at Swimming Pool
EXT. Rear Theater Alley to curb – Both modern and period 1927
EXT. Sidestreet and Speakeasy steps

THE TWILIGHT ZONE – "The Trouble With Templeton"

Rev. 10/30/60

1. INT BEDROOM   WIDE ANGLE SHOT   DAY

The CAMERA is at the dressing-room end of an elaborate area which functions as a study and a bedroom for a man. At this dressing room end there is an arrangement of sliding doors of the built-in wardrobe closets not unlike those found in a haberdashery. Two or three doors are open, revealing racks of suits and topcoats and shoes and shelf after shelf of shirts and other linens.

The bathroom door opens and BOOTH TEMPLETON steps into the room. Although Templeton is tieless at the moment and his collar is open, he is distinguished and impressive, an extraordinarily handsome man near sixty with a fine profile and even features.

He comes across the room walking directly toward the CAMERA, stops in the extreme CLOSE SHOT and reaches beyond the CAMERA swinging back a door that contains rack after rack of ties.

2. CLOSE ANGLE   BOOTH TEMPLETON

He snaps on an indirect light and studies the selection of ties. As he does this unhurriedly and with care we notice that his shirt is monogrammed, that his links are expensive and in perfect taste, that his suit trousers are well tailored, that his carefully trimmed moustache and perfect barbering – indeed everything about him—stamp his as a man who takes an exceptional interest in his personal appearance.

At length Templeton dwarfs his selection to two ties, takes them off the rack, studies them in the light, makes an irritable gesture, then steps across the room toward the window and the daylight.

3. SHOT BY WINDOW

This light is still not proper since it is filtered by frosted glass. Templeton unlatches the catch and screws the window back allowing a dull, grey daylight to enter so that he can study the ties and make a selection.

3. CONTINUED

It is still not satisfactory since it is not so much the lighting that is faulty but Templeton's eyes. Perhaps there is furtiveness that suggests vanity in the way he slips a pair of foldups (glasses) from his pocket, fits them on and resumes his problem. A burst of female laughter invades harshly from the outside; and this is quickly followed by a man's answering laughter. Templeton glances out the window.

4. EXT TEMPLETON'S HOME   WHAT HE SEES   DAY

The ANGLE LOOKS DOWN from the window onto the side area of the home. There is an expensive foreign car parked there in back of a sleek limousine. Beyond this there is an arrangement of gardens and landscaping that compliment the swimming pool. DORIS TEMPLETON and ED PAGE are standing by the pool, drying off after a swim. Doris is a flagrantly attractive bitch of thirty or so and Page is tall and black-shocked, a wearer of burly sweaters and a driver of foreign cars. They're cozy enough laughing at their private joke completely engrossed in one another. It comes across in the easy kind of familiarity Doris has with Page's hand and in Page's whispering close in her ear—causing her to shriek with laughter once more.

5. INT BEDROOM   CLOSE ANGLE   TEMPLETON DAY

Templeton stares outside with a patient tiredness as Doris' laughter dies o.s. and conversation replaces it.

>MARTY (O.S.)
>Good morning, Mr. Templeton.

Templeton turns with the CAMERA to face Marty—a gentle-looking man, immaculate in a chauffer's black uniform—who comes up quietly with a glass of water in hand.

>TEMPLETON
>Our new guest this week…his name is what?

>MARTY
>That is Mr. Page, sir. Mr. Edward Page.

                    TEMPLETON
            Page. Page Page. Yes. Has he been here
            before?

                    MARTY
            No, sir, he's new.

Their eyes lock momentarily. Marty produces a small silver pill box—Templeton looks at the pills.

                    TEMPLETON
            And these are new, too?

                    MARTY
            Yes, sir. On the hour, every hour, Mr. Templeton.

Templeton takes a pill from the proffered box, then glances out the window again hearing more laughter.

                    TEMPLETON
            Missus Templeton's not very discreet these days,
            is she?

It's a statement, not a question. Marty follows his gaze.

6. EXT TEMPLETON'S HOME   WHAT THEY SEE   DAY

Doris and Page are still near the pool. Doris has one arm loosely flung about Page's waist. There'll be damn little swimming pool.

7. INT BEDROOM-STUDY   CLOSE ANGLE   MARTY &
    TEMPLETON

Templeton stares out the window. Marty looks at him painfully.

                    TEMPLETON
            The discreetness was an early fatality, it lasted
            such a very short time.

Templeton sighs, turns away, trades Marty the ties for the glass of water. But he does not take the pill right away—instead he weighs it in his hand.

                    TEMPLETON
          I suppose she's waiting for the day when one of
          these won't do what it was designed to do. And
          perhaps…I'm waiting for that day, too.

Marty makes a solicitous noise.

                    MARTY
          Please, sir…

                    TEMPLETON
          Don't distress yourself, old friend.

Templeton plops the pill in his mouth, washes it down quickly, hands the glass back to Marty. He takes his ties back from Marty, selects hurriedly, hands one tie back to Marty and sets the other one in place under his collar and removes his foldup glasses.

                    TEMPLETON
          When a man my age marries a woman her age,
          he gets exactly what he deserves. I'm old, Marty.

Templeton steps away from the window back toward the dressing room area.

8. ANOTHER ANGLE

Templeton moves in front of a full length mirror that is lined with a series of ornate tiers on which there are statuettes, figurines, clocks, and other bric-a-brac. Templeton buttons his collar and begins tying his tie carefully. Marty comes up, replaces the tie, saying:

                    MARTY
          Mr. Templeton, you could never be old.

Templeton gives his a wry smile.

                    TEMPLETON
          Old. And getting older even as we stand here
          speaking.

9. REFLECTION SHOT   FROM MIRROR

Templeton adjusting his tie, fitting it carefully.

                TEMPLETON
        They say—or at least they've said it in most of
        my plays—that when a man achieves years, he
        achieves reason and contentment.
                (pause; ruefully)
        I haven't.

A renewed flurry of laughter from the outside jerks Templeton's attention in that direction of the window. Marty glances o.s. uneasily.

                MARTY
        Mr. Templeton, sir, may I suggest that possibly
        this isn't the day for you to go down there? Perhaps
        I could telephone the theatre and explain that you
        won't be able to start rehearsals…

Templeton looks at him fondly.

                TEMPLETON
        Thank you, Marty, but I'll go down *there*…

Templeton spreads one hand on a briefcase lying atop the dresser before him.

                TEMPLETON
        …I'll rehearse *this* play and *it* will open.

Templeton looks back at the mirror and makes a fingertip inspection of his hairline.

                TEMPLETON
        And on that night a succession of makeup men
        will dye what hair I have left and supply me
        with what hair I need.

He begins to fit a collar ornament under his tie.

> TEMPLETON
> The director will show me my lines and the stage
> Manager will show me my place…and when it's over
> They'll say, "Wonderful, Mr. Templeton."

The collar ornament is statisfactory, Templeton now fits a tie clasp into place.

> TEMPLETON
> Then the stage manager will see to it that I'm
> properly delivered to you – so that you can properly
> deliver me back here – so that I'll be able to go back
> there and do the same thing the next night.
> (indicates window)
> I won't see or particularly care what's going on
> out there…or anywhere in this house. I'll just
> want to go to bed, Marty. That's the best place
> for me. Bed. Sleep. Oblivion.

Marty picks up Templeton's suit coat with a painful look.

> TEMPLETON
> It doesn't matter. I don't love her anymore. I can
> remember when I did…but I can't recall a single,
> separated contented moment of it.
> (pause, then huskily)
> There haven't been many contented moments
> In my life, Marty…but I can recall some…long ago…

Templeton glances to his left, slightly above eye level.

10. REVERSE ANGLE TIGHT EFFECT SHOT

The outline of an ornate music box resting among the bric-a-brac on the tiers, fills part of the frame.

10. CONTINUED

Templeton reaches up gingerly, touching it as men touch those things they love best.

                    TEMPLETON
                (softly)
            Laura.

Templeton trips the mechanism. The figurine begins to revolve, the MUSIC comes over gently. Templeton's eyes water.

                    TEMPLETON
                (softly)
            The freshest, most radiant lady God ever made.
            Eighteen when we were married, Marty,
            twenty-five when she died. Why did He have
            to take her away from me?

Marty pushes his face in SHOT.

                    MARTY
            Mr. Templeton! Please! Don't do this to yourself,
            please, sir!

But Templeton is watching the music box, nods his head, humming softly with the music...

                    TEMPLETON
            Some moments in life have an indescribable
            loveliness to them. Those moments I had
            with Laura...
                (a realization)
            ...they're all that's left for me.
            You understand that, Marty?

                    MARTY
                (moved)
            Yes, sir, I believe I do, sir, Mr. Templeton, but
            Mr. Templeton, you...I...

Templeton looks at him now. Marty's old face is stricken with sympathy. Templeton clicks off the Music box, touches Marty on the arm.

                    TEMPLETON
            I'm alright, old friend, I'm quite alright.

11. ANOTHER ANGLE

Marty is not convinced but he helps Templeton slip into his suit coat. While Templeton buttons this carefully, Marty gets his other things ready, scarf, hat, and gloves. He hands these items to Templeton one at a time. Templeton sets the hat carefully on his head, places the scarf about his shoulders, then allows Marty to help him into his topcoat. After he has buttoned this carefully, he draws on his gloves. All of this is done in front of the mirror, carefully and unhurriedly.

                    SERLING'S VOICE (O.S.)
Pleased to present for your consideration Mr. Booth Templeton, serious and successful star of over thirty Broadway plays—who is not quite alright today. More precisely—today is not quite alright for Booth Templeton. Yesterday and its memories is what he wants; and yesterday is what he'll get.

Templeton is ready. Marty scoops up his own topcoat and opens the door. Templeton picks up his briefcase and steps through. Marty follows. CAMERA SWINGS to the window, where SERLING stands.

                    SERLING
Soon his years and his troubles will descent upon him in an avalanche. In order not to be crushed, Mr. Booth Templeton will escape from his theatre and his world and make his debut on another stage in another world that we call—The Twilight Zone.

FADE OUT:

OPENING BILLBOARD

FIRST COMMERCIAL

FADE IN:

12. EXT SIGN UP ANGLE   DAY

The sign reads simply: Empire Theatre Stage Entrance. Traffic SOUNDS come o.s. Among them, a car drawing to a halt nearby.

13. EXT NEW YORK STREET AT ALLEY   WIDE ANGLE SHOT
DAY

Here is what might be called a traditional New York theatre alley and surrounding area. Marty halts the gleaming black limousine at the curbing, hops out with briefcase in hand and opens the rear door. Templeton steps out.

14. ANOTHER ANGLE   REAR OF THEATRE

Templeton's arrival is of interest to a bulldog of a man in homburg and chesterfield who is keeping vigil near the stage door. A tooth pick chewer is SIDNEY SPERRY, one the best, he uses it like an antenna to test the air, the people and God.

15. SHOT BY LIMOUSINE

Marty closes the door and hands Templeton the briefcase. Templeton heads for the stair. Marty climbs back in the car to wait.

16. SHOT AT DOOR

Templeton approaches the door and Sperry extends a thick hand. We are aware of a series of billboard posters at the sides of the door.

                SPERRY
          (familiarly)
       You're late, Booth.

Templeton looks at him vaguely.

                SPERRY
       After twelve.
         (jerks a thumb indicating inside)
       Boy wonder won't like it, kiddo.

Sperry moves over, opens the door. Templeton starts inside...pauses.

              TEMPLETON
      Who is the boy wonder...?

                SPERRY
      Arthur Willis. Directing.

> TEMPLETON
> Oh…you must be mistaken. Duff Meager is our director.

> SPERRY
> *Was.* Canned him last night. We need someone who'll give it some zip, pep. Not my racket but I know what's good and what's bad as well as the next guy—and I wanted to come by this morning and let everyone know I'm personally interested in this thing. Art Willis is okay with you, isn't he?

> TEMPLETON
> I've heard of him, of course, but I've never actually met him, Mr. Uh….

> SPERRY
> I'm Sid Sperry, Booth. My money is backing this play. Don't you remember?

Templeton doesn't recall yet.

> TEMPLETON
> Oh…oh, yes, of course, Mr. Sperry. I'm rather forgetful when it comes to names. Always have been.

Sperry claps Templeton on the back.

> SPERRY
> S'okay! Just so's you don't forget your lines.

This possibility has haunted Templeton for a long time. He gives Sperry a sharp look and moves on inside. Sperry follows.

17. INT. THEATRE BACK STAGE   PAN WITH TEMPLETON AND SPERRY

The two men move inside now, into a dimly lit area which reveals a mass of backstage paraphernalia. CAMERA moves just behind them, and we see with them a rehearsal piano, set pieces, hanging ropes, dresses on a wardrobe rack. These are obstructions to their view, and our view, of the stage itself, but between the objects we catch quick glimpses of a rehearsal table, center stage, actors seated at the table and director Arthur Willis intoning what is now and unrecognizable walla. Templeton and Sperry come to a clear view of the stage. Presumably Templeton will walk straight to the table. But to Sperry's surprise, the actor continues to walk down the side of the backstage area, doing anything to delay his appearance. They pass more set pieces, a section of a staircase and now arrive in the wings. They turn. With them, we can look out on stage and see the table. They hear the Tennessee accent of director Willis.

> WILLIS
> ...I'll say this once, just once and only once, but I'll expect each and every one of you to understand it.

18-19. SHOT OF STAGE   THEIR POV

Willis, an irritated young man, is standing at the head of a long table. The CAST of the play are arranged about the table listening to his every word. The rest of the stage is barren, in comparative darkness like the seating section, but Arthur Willis knows his effects. He stands directly under a single overhead light that emphasizes his extreme youth, his sharp angular figure and his bony, lean face.

20. TWO SHOT   TEMPLETON AND SPERRY

Staring toward the stage. Templeton recoils visibly. Sperry gives him a smug glance that is accompanied by a toothpick adjustment.

21. CLOSE SHOT   WILLIS

His words come out biting, acid-like.

> WILLIS
> Michael Frantz is producing this play.
> Mr. Coombs has written it.
> You have been *hired* to act in it—
> I have been *contracted* to direct it.

Willis's SECRETARY, a horsy-looking dame in horned rims materializes at his side, waiting patiently for her chance to convey some urgent message to her God.

> WILLIS
> So. Make no mistake about what we are here to do and make no mistake about me!

22. TWO SHOT   TEMPLETON AND SPERRY

Templeton has removed his gloves and his scarf but pauses, unbuttoning his coat, staring fascinated at the workings of Willis's mouth.

23. BIG CLOSEUP   WILLIS'S MOUTH

His lips moving tightly as he speaks.

>   WILLIS
> I will direct this play *my* way at *all* times—
> is that clearly understood?

Willis pauses for emphasis fixing and eye on each member of the cast. The Secretary takes his opportunity to push into the SHOT and whisper her urgent message into his ear. Whatever she is saying irritates him still more.

24. TWO SHOT   TEMPLETON AND SPERRY

Sperry's toothpick clucks up and down approvingly.

>   SPERRY
>   (low)
> Like that, like that very much.
> In control that boy, right from the start.
> Give us a good play.

>   TEMPLETON
>   (mechanically)
> Us...?

Sperry's toothpick looks irritated – no one forgets his name twice.

>   SPERRY
>   (tightly)
> *Sperry*, Templeton, *Sperry!*

>   TEMPLETON
> Mr. Sperry. Yes. I apologize. That's impolite
> of me. I shan't forget again.

Sperry glowers darkly, his toothpick stageward.

>WILLIS (O.S.)
>Call his home! Call his home!

The voice is shrill with authority and anger; they look.

27. MEDIUM SHOT ON STAGE

Willis has just checked his watch—which irritates him more than ever. The Secretary is scurrying away to carry out his order. Then Willis' gaze happens to go to the wings.

>WILLIS
>Never mind, Valencia!

The secretary stops.

28. TWO SHOT   TEMPLETON AND SPERRY

Sperry nudges him.

29. CLOSE SHOT   WILLIS

Willis steps away from the table, addressing his cast with a sweeping gesture.

>WILLIS
>(acidly)
>Some of us are young, some of us are old, but neither state precludes any of us, young or old, from ignoring the basic cooperation that will be necessary here! (he turns around and about as he speaks, maneuvering toward the wings) when I direct, there are no significant personalities in the cast of a play—but there are three significant dates in the Life of a play!
>(wheels and looks directly at Templeton)

30. TWO SHOT   TEMPLETON AND SPERRY

Sperry's mouth and toothpick make a grimace; Templeton recoils slightly.

31. SHOT PAST TEMPLETON TO WILLIS

Willis is at the edge of the wings now, spreadlegged and formidable.

> WILLIS
> The first day of rehearsal! Opening night! closing night! The last two are related and dependent on the first one! Therefore, the first day of rehearsal is an extremely important date! When I called rehearsal for twelve o'clock, Templeton, I meant *twelve* o'clock for *everyone*— young and old—everyone to be in his place and ready to work at twelve o'clock sharp!

32. EFFECT SHOT   TEMPLETON

He stares back bewilderedly, then for no reason gives Sperry a helpless look.

33. FULL SHOT

All eyes are on Templeton now. Willis points at him dramatically.

> WILLIS
> (sarcastically)
> Are you ready to work with us, Templeton?

34. EFFECT SHOT   SPERRY

Looking at Templeton sideways, working his toothpick around on his tongue, enjoying Templeton's dismay.

35. EFFECT SHOT   TEMPLETON

Perspiration on his forehead, trembling slightly.

> WILLIS (O.S.)
> I asked you a question, Templeton! I expect an answer!

He moves down to steps into the SHOT.

                            WILLIS
                      Answer me! Answer me!

Templeton gulps, swallows, unable to speak.

36. FLASH SHOT   SPERRY

The toothpick has stopped moving, suspended now on his tongue—waiting for Templeton to do something.

37. ANGLE FAVORING TEMPLETON

Willis presses closer.

                            WILLIS
                   Speak up, Templeton, speak up!

Templeton drops his briefcase and the script spills out. He looks at Willis, at Sperry, at the Cast, makes a movement to pick up the script, then suddenly lets out an anguished cry and turns away, heading rapidly toward the rear stage door.

38. POV FROM STAGE DOOR AREA

Templeton begins to run toward the CAMERA. Willis is pursuing.

                            WILLIS
                 Templeton! Templeton! Come back here!

39. EFFECT ANGLE

Templeton tries the stage door. Voices and pounding feet are heading for him. He grabs the door handle just as Willis, Sperry, the Secretary burst into view.

                            WILLIS
                         Templeton!

Templeton jerks open the door and plunges through.

CUT TO:

40. EXT. REAR OF THEATRE MEDIUM CLOSE ANGLE   NIGHT
Templeton plunges out the door, then sags against the wall, weak with exertion and emotion. He takes out his handkerchief and mops his face – then reacts slightly hearing a faint scattering of polite applause.

40A. REVERSE ANGLE

A small group of people are gathered at the stage entrance, applauding politely. Templeton takes no notice that the women are dressed in the flagrant styling of 1927, nor that the men wear straw hats and crimp-cut suits and wing collars with their dinner jackets. They seem like pleasant enough people—too pleasant for Templeton—since it's obvious that the applause is spontaneous in his direction—along with the AD LIBS. "Wonderful show" "Fine evening in the theatre" "Excellent performance." Templeton doesn't know that to make of it—and really doesn't want to make anything of it. He works his way past them as best he can, intent on the refuge of his car. He doesn't notice that the alley is considerably different than when he entered a few minutes before or that it is suddenly night where it had been day.

41. WIDE ANGLE ON STREET

Templeton plunges toward the black car parked at the curbing. He does not notice that it is of 1927 vintage. But when he puts his hand on the door to climb in, it suddenly starts up and drives away.

                    TEMPLETON
          What!

And then he reacts.

42. INSERT LICENSE PLATE ON MOVING CAR

It is genuine enough but reads: NEW YORK STATE – 1927

44. BACK TO TEMPLETON

He doesn't know what to make of it. Another 1926 or 1927 model draws up. He turns in confusion.

46. TEMPLETON'S POV   SHOT TOWARD THEATRE WALL

We see a row of posters. Templeton moves toward them.

46A. CLOSE ON FIRST POSTER

It reads: "NOW APPEARING MR. BOOTH TEMPLETON IN 'THE GREAT SEED'" Across the legend a sticker has been slapped. It reads "1927's BIG HIT."

> TEMPLETON'S VOICE OVER
> "Booth Templeton in The Great Seed! 1927's Big Hit! More than thirty years ago..."

46B. BACK TO TEMPLETON CLOSE

Confused and frightened. He moves to second poster.

46C. CLOSE ON SECOND POSTER

It reads: "The Great Seed" Written and directed by Barney Flueger" Across the legend the same 1927 sticker has been slapped.

> TEMPLETON'S VOICE OVER
> "Barney!" "Barney!"

46D. BACK TO TEMPLETON CLOSE

He touches the poster, as if he expected it to crumble or disappear as if it were a mirage.

46E. CLOSE ON THIRD POSTER

It reads "The Great Seed" Critics acclaim it! Public acclaims it! The same 1927 legend is across it.

46F. BACK TO TEMPLETON CLOSE

He is stunned. He turns around, lost. A passerby stares at him, assuming he is drunk.

                    EDDIE'S VOICE
                Hey, Mr. Templeton!

Templeton looks up.

51. EXT. STAGE DOOR – CLOSE ON EDDIE

Eddie, the doorman, moves quickly to Templeton.

                    TEMPLETON
                What year is this?

                    EDDIE
                You trying to kid me, Mr. Templeton?

                    TEMPLETON
                Most assuredly I am not.

                    EDDIE
                Your wife just phoned and said you were to meet
                her at Freddie Iacino's.

                    TEMPLETON
                Wife...? Laura's dead!

                    EDDIE
                She's the best looking ghost I've seen tonight!
                No offense, Mr. Templeton!

Templeton's face has clouded, he grabs Eddie by the shoulders, trembling with anticipation.

                    TEMPLETON
                Where's Laura? Where's she waiting for me?

                    EDDIE
                Freddie Iacino's. Right around the corner!

Templeton turns to the CAMERA, his face elated with anticipation. The CAMERA MOVES FORWARD and the screen goes to BLACK.

FADE OUT

FADE IN:

52. EXT DARK SIDE STREET ESTABLISHING SHOT   HIGH CAMERA   NIGHT

It is a rundown, shabby area of darkened brownstones and tenement buildings, dimly-lit and apparently deserted – until we see Templeton rounding the corner under a squirt of streetlight and running down the street.

53. LONG SHOT   TEMPLETON

Running, his topcoat flapping about his legs. He comes into the CLOSE SHOT, halts abruptly, panting—and looking at the three steps which lead down to a dark doorway.

He moves forward.

54. CLOSE ANGLE BY DOORWAY

Templeton moves down the steps, hesitates then presses the buzzer on the door.

We hear a bolt being shot, a latch clicks, and the door opens eight inches.

55. SHOT PAST TEMPLETON

FREDDIE IACINO, a swarthy man in shirtsleeves peers out cautiously. Behind him we can see a short, narrow hallway with a sickly light burning above another door at the far end.

                    TEMPLETON
            (awed)
      Freddie!

                    FREDDIE
      Hello, Booth.

Freddie jerks his head—opens the door indicating Templeton should enter. Templeton steps through.

56. INT SHORT HALLWAY   MEDIUM CLOSE ANGLE   NIGHT

Templeton stands, amazed, watching Freddie close the door, replace the latch, return the bolt. Freddie turns to him.

>   FREDDIE
>   (edgy)
>   Gotta be too careful these days, alla time
>   somebody's wanting a raid or something.

56. CONTINUED

Templeton touches his shoulder.

Freddie gives him a strange look.

>   FREDDIE
>   Yeah...what?

>   TEMPLETON
>   It *is* you. You're...alive.

>   FREDDIE
>   Sure.

57. INT SPEAKEASY   NIGHT   FULL SHOT

It is a small room, dimly lit and fairly well crowded. Some patrons are at the bar; others are seated at tables and booths. A small band is on the stage playing a mellow "Moonlight on The Ganges"

Templeton steps in with Freddie, the Negro closes the door and takes up his impassive-faced vigil behind them. Templeton looks about, his face registering incredibility.

>   FREDDIE
>   Steaks or chops?

>   TEMPLETON
>   Huh?

                         FREDDIE
                Your wife's having the Kansas City.

Templeton looks—almost fearfully beyond Freddie.

58. WHAT HE SEES

A vacant booth in the rear away from the crowd and the noise. A candle burns on the table, two places are set, but no one is there.

59. CLOSE ANGLE   TEMPLETON AND FREDDIE

Templeton registers dismay.

                         TEMPLETON
                  She isn't at our old table!

Freddie nudges him, indicates another area. Templeton looks.

60. WHAT HE SEES

LAURA TEMPLETON is seated at a table near the bandstand eating and talking rapidly with BARNEY FLUEGER who's back is to the CAMERA.

Laura is quite lovely and vivacious, possessing that fresh brightness that somehow goes with a child and every bit the soft and lovely woman of memory—but also another woman, too. Dressed in a beaded gown, coiffeured alla 1927, there is a crisp urgent hardness about her that is very unlike that memory.

Barney Flueger, if we could see him, would prove to be a vital, dynamic man with slick hair dressed in a dark jacket, white flannels, and an ascot.

61. CLOSE ANGLE   TEMPLETON AND FREDDIE

Templeton's face softens staring across the crowded room at Laura.

                         FREDDIE
                    Well...?

Freddie has his order book out.

                    FREDDIE
          Steaks or chops?

                    TEMPLETON
          Nothing….nothing to eat tonight, Freddie.
          We aren't staying very long.

                    FREDDIE
          Suit yourself.

Freddie moves off. Templeton pats down his hair, straightens his coat, adjusts his tie. Then moves forward.

62. SHOT AT TABLE   LAURA AND BARNEY

Barney and Laura are conversing in low tones completely engrossed in each other. Suddenly Laura pauses with a forkful of steak in midair, throws back her head and laughs shrilly. Barney gets to his feet.

                    LAURA
          You're a scream, Barney, a real scream!
                    (claps him on the back)
          But I wouldn't dare tell that kind
          Of story to anyone—not even my husband—

Templeton steps into SHOT with eyes only for her. Laura looks at him casually.

                    LAURA
                    (breezily)
          Hi.

Barney turns.

                    BARNEY
          Hi, Booth, we didn't wait!

Templeton reacts seeing Barney.

                    TEMPLETON
          Barney! Barney Flueger!

Barney claps Templeton on the back.

>BARNEY
>The same. To know him is to love him.
>Sit down, old chap. Be right back.

Barney moves off quickly…Templeton stares at Laura, trembling with eagerness.

>TEMPLETON
>Laura! Laura, darling!

Templeton bends to kiss her and in the act tries awkwardly to embrace her. Neither things work—she is sitting; he is standing. Laura pushes his him away, glancing around slightly embarrassed.

>LAURA
>My goodness, Booth!

Laura pats the chair next to her.

Templeton sits down beside her, his eyes devouring her hungrily. He starts to take her hand but she uses it to put steak in her mouth.

>LAURA
>Kansas City's great, tonight, honey. Juicy!
>>(giggles, wipes her chin)
>I toldja.

>TEMPLETON
>Laura, I…

Laura concentrates on carving off another chunk of meat.

>LAURA
>Something the matter, honey? You look worried.
>Why didn't you take off your makeup?

>TEMPLETON
>Makeup…?

Then his hand goes to his face, realizing how old he must look to her. This isn't working out quite right for Templeton. He leans nearer her chair.

> **TEMPLETON**
> Let's get out of here, Laura, go someplace
> Where it's quieter and there aren't so many people.

> **LAURA**
> (flatly)
> Why?

> **TEMPLETON**
> I want to talk to you, Laura!

> **LAURA**
> I want to have a good time!

Laura looks offstage at a passing waiter and squeals.

> **LAURA**
> Yoo-hoo!

Laura picks up her empty beer schooner.

> **LAURA**
> (to waiter)
> Wouldja get me one more of these, please?
> Please, thank you kindly.

The waiter nods and moves off.

> **TEMPLETON**
> I *have* to talk to you, Laura.

She looks at him blandly, waiting for him to say something. He can't speak.

> **LAURA**
> Well...?

                    TEMPLETON
            I...Laura, I'm here.
                    (she nods)
            Laura—I don't know for how long, or even how I
            got here, or who put me here, but I'm here and I
            want to make use of the time—I want to have you
            alone—to myself—I—

Laura looks slightly exasperated.

                    LAURA
            Oh, Booth! Don't be dull.

63. ANOTHER ANGLE

Barney has moved back into SHOT with a manuscript in hand which he casually tosses onto the table as he seats himself.

                    BARNEY
                    (nods)
            New band's swell.
                    (to Booth)
            Aren't you going to eat, old chap?

Barney brandishes his knife and fork and tears into his steak. Laura is doing the same. Templeton looks puzzledly from one to the other.

64. TIGHT ANGLE AT TABLE

Laura and Barney are eating ravenously. Templeton watches them a moment, then...

                    TEMPLETON
            Laura...Barney...

Barney looks up.

                    BARNEY
            Better order.

                    LAURA
            He's right, honey.

                    TEMPLETON
               (a little desperately)
        Listen to me…you two….

They pause, looking at him. The Waiter reappears, plunks the beer in front of Laura. Laura grabs for it eagerly.

                     BARNEY
                   (to waiter)
        Bring him….
                 (indicating Booth)
        …one a' these.
                 (indicating his steak)

The waiter nods, moves off. Laura finishes a long draft of beer, plunks the glass down, picks up a manuscript on the table and begins fanning herself impatiently:

                     LAURA
        Phew…we…so hot tonight…will I be glad to
        get into a cold tub…phew…wee…
                 (looks at Templeton)
        Would you tell me whatever reason on this glad,
        green earth you are wearing a topcoat for on a
        night like this? Would you please tell me, Booth!
                   (to Barney)
        Now I ask you. *Really*.

Barney chuckles.

                    TEMPLETON
        I'm not so certain this is a glad, green earth!

Laura pauses with her fanning—looks at Barney.

                    TEMPLETON
        Laura…darling. Barney, I'm not so certain of this
        earth or anything in it right now, I…

She begins to fan herself again. Templeton stops her hand.

TEMPLETON
Please...listen to me. Something's happened, Laura, something very strange. Try to understand...this
(touches his face)
...isn't makeup. In another world...for many lonely years I've had nothing but a memory of you to live on, Laura...and you, too, Barney, you were my one and only best friend...but both of you have been only memories for a long time. And now...tonight or today...whatever it is and wherever I am in time and space...somehow...some way I have you back again—you're alive. You didn't die. Life's going on here...just as if you didn't die. Either of you. Can you understand that?

Laura says nothing. Templeton looks at Barney. Barney nods.

BARNEY
Sure.

Barney starts with his steak again. Templeton looks at Laura.

TEMPLETON
Laura...? Do *you* understand?

Laura shrugs.

LAURA
Sure! Let's have some fun!

She reaches for her glass.

TEMPLETON
Laura! Why are you so different?

LAURA
This is the way I am, this is the way it is. What did you expect?

He stares at her incredibly. Then turns as Barney asks:

                    BARNEY
            Yeah, old chap, what *did* you expect?

                    TEMPLETON
            I...I don't know.
                    (turns to Laura desperately)
            You were my love! Everywhere...at
            all times! We couldn't walk a street or sit in a restaurant
            without everyone knowing we were in love...
            we...

Laura's face remains faintly hard. But a —

65. FLASH SHOT OF BARNEY

...shows him to be intent, earnest.

66. ANOTHER ANGLE

Laura shrugs impatiently.

                    LAURA
            Are you finished?

                    TEMPLETON
            I...don't like what you've become!

Laura suddenly breaks out laughing, pointing at Templeton. Barney throws back his head and laughs uproariously.

Templeton stands, turns on Barney savagely, raking glasses off the table.

                    TEMPLETON
            Shut up! Shut up, I tell you, shut up!

Barney shuts up. Templeton looks desperately from Barney to Laura.

                    TEMPLETON
            Laura, please...come with me and...

Laura gets to her feet looking at him gravely, she still has the manuscript in hand.

                            LAURA
                         (coldly)
                You're a silly, old fool of a man!

Suddenly, without warning the MUSIC starts up o.s. loud and brash and fast. Laura brightens instantly.

                            LAURA
                       That's for me!

67. WIDE ANGLE

Shows the band playing. Laura extends her arms and starts for the dance floor.

                          TEMPLETON
                     Wait…no…please…

Laura laughs and begins dancing, wiggles and giggles and squeals and whirls the beads on her dress flying around. Other patrons applaud.

68. ANOTHER ANGLE

Templeton watches the exhibition in dismay.

                          TEMPLETON
                         No…no…

Then he looks at Barney. Barney grins broadly and yells:

                           BARNEY
                       Attaway, baby!

69. EFFECT SHOT   LAURA

Dancing wildly. Templeton can stand it no longer. He moves into the SHOT and grabs her roughly—pulls her to him.

                          TEMPLETON
                    Stop it, Laura! Stop it!

Laura slaps him across the face with the manscript, angrily. He grabs it from her hand. ALL MUSIC STOPS, all eyes upon them.

                    LAURA
          Why don't you go back where you came from.
          We don't want you here!

Her face is a mask of fury.

70. FLASH SHOT   TEMPLETON

Reacting.

71. FLASH SHOT   BARNEY

Who has jumped to his feet. Templeton looks at him helplessly. Barney grins evilly.

72. ANOTHER ANGLE

Templeton studies the sea of faces around him—then turns his back on Laura and heads for the doorway.
Barney comes up to stand alongside Laura.

73. ANOTHER ANGLE

Templeton walks directly into the CAMERA, swings the door back and EXITS behind the CAMERA and suddenly we are viewing the entire room - and particularly the faces of Barney and Laura.

74. EFFECT SHOT

Their faces are suddenly soft and compassionate, as a re the faces of all the others in the room who have suddenly ceased their actions. Then the room begins to be swallowed in a blackness and the last face we see is Laura's strained with an overwhelming sadness.

LAP DISSOLVE:

75. EXT THE REAR OF THEATRE   FULL SHOT   NIGHT

The street and the theatre are all darkened now. Templeton comes in to SHOT quickly—a dazed, broken, tired man, he looks back over his shoulder once, then pulls open the door.

76. INT THEATRE BACK STAGE   CLOSE ANGLE   DAY

Templeton comes back into the chaotic comfort of back stage, pauses, leans back against the door, closes his eyes which are wet with tears. He stands like that a long moment in his agony and then he opens his eyes, aware of distant voices.

77. TEMPLETON'S POV   LONG SHOT

On the stage he can see Willis and Sperry and the members of the cast. He moves toward stage. It is Willis who looks up—nods—and others look toward the rear area, toward the approaching actor.

78. CLOSE ANGLE   TEMPLETON

He reacts, then registers bewilderment.

                    TEMPLETON
        Did it happen, or…

78. CONTINUED

Templeton brings his hand up to his face—then his eyes widen. He still has the manuscript in his hand.
He stares down at it…staring.

79. INSERT   THE TITLE

It reads: "WHAT TO DO WHEN BOOTH COMES BACK" by Barney Flueger. Templeton's hand moves into SHOT; opens the page.

                  TEMPLETON'S VOICE
       What to do when Booth comes back.

80. CLOSE ANGLE   TEMPLETON

reading quickly.

                    TEMPLETON
       Table in Speakeasy. Enter Booth as Laura
       throws back her head and laughs too shrilly.
       "You're a scream, Barney, a real…"

Templeton flips over to another page…

> TEMPLETON
> Barney: The same. To know his is to love him.
> Sit down, old chap…

And still another page.

> TEMPLETON
> Laura: Why don't you go back where you came from. We don't want you here?

Templeton looks up from the manuscript, his face filling with wonder.

> TEMPLETON
> Acting! They were *acting*…for me!
> They wanted me to come back to my own life…and *live* it!

He straightens up and the tiredness and depression seem to drop from him as the spirit of what he has just experienced begins to take hold.

> WILLIS (o.s.)
> Templeton…?

Templeton looks up to face him.

81. WIDE ANGLE SHOT

Willis wears a smug look of triumph flanked by Sperry and his Secretary. Other cast members hang in the b.g.

> WILLIS
> One question…are you in or are you out?

Templeton takes his time, looks them over slowly and then smiles faintly.

> TEMPLETON
> I am definitely…in. And it is definitely *Mister* Templeton…

                    WILLIS
          Ha?

                    TEMPLETON
          ...especially to one so young as yourself.

                    WILLIS
          Now just a minute...

                    TEMPLETON
                    (cutting through)
          Excuse me, Mr. Sperry. I never allow
          anyone not directly connected with the
          production to attend rehearsals.

Sperry's toothpick halts in amazement.

                    TEMPLETON
                    (to Willis)
          I *insist* on that.

Willis blanches, then mumbles.

                    WILLIS
          Run along, Sidney.

                    SPERRY
          What's...?

Sperry thinks better of protesting, turns and exits shot. Templeton starts off toward the rehearsal area.

                    TEMPLETON
          Now then, shall we begin rehearsal?

81. CONTINUED

Willis decides he'd better do just that. He moves to catch up with Templeton.

                    WILLIS
          I'd like to, Mr. Templeton.

When Willis catches up, Templeton talks as he walks, easy and commandingly.

> TEMPLETON
> I've just had a most remarkable experience,
> young man. I couldn't possibly expect that
> you would comprehend it, but I am going to
> tell you about it anyway. Someday.
> (pause)
> You know, Arthur, the first day of rehearsal *is*
> the most important date in the life of a play.

82. LONG ANGLE

As they walk toward the table followed by the Cast, the CAMERA MOVES to a HIGH ANGLE. The Cast assembles on the stage. Templeton takes his seat at the table. Then others sit down. Willis nods politely and the first reading of the play gets under way.

OVER THIS WE HEAR:

> NARRATOR'S VOICE (o.s.)
> Booth Templeton the actor, once more alive and
> once more a part of his world…a man who found
> out that a memory is a precious thing not to
> be tampered with…even in…The Twilight Zone.

FADE OUT

<u>THE END</u>

OCEE RITCH
"Dead Man's Shoes"

The only known script written for television by OCee Ritch (1922-1981) is "Dead Man's Shoes," screen-credited entirely to Charles Beaumont. Beaumont was growing increasingly busy with writing assignments at the time; he had a small number of colleagues ghost-write for him, against the rules of the Writers Guild of America. Ritch previously generated the story for Beaumont's second season *Twilight Zone* episode "Static," a tale about a magical radio.

Ritch was a member of the so-called Southern California Group of writers, which consisted of Beaumont, Ray Bradbury, John Tomerlin, George Clayton Johnson, William F. Nolan, Richard Matheson, and others. Members of this group also had an affinity for automobiles and auto racing; Ritch was a car enthusiast and expert. From approximately 1960 to 1980, he wrote dozens of articles for automotive magazines and manuals, in addition to many short stories.

Beaumont's 1963 compilation of essays, *Remember, Remember?* was dedicated in part to Ritch, who contributed to some of the pieces in the book. He also ghost-wrote several articles for *Playboy* for Beaumont and appeared in Beaumont's 1961 feature film "The Intruder."

The script's working title was "The Reluctant Genius," and the featured item was a cowboy hat.

"Dead Man's Shoes" has a solid storyline but the television episode is not generally remembered or discussed, probably because of its oddly nondescript characters and unusual development as a cycle. A bowery bum, Nate Bledsoe, swipes some two-toned loafers off a dead gangster lying in an alley. In so doing, he unknowingly steps into the dead man's soul.

"Dead Man's Shoes" bears some similarity to the ending of Serling's "What You Need." Steve Cochran, who plays a greasy middle-aged loser, meets an elderly clairvoyant sidewalk peddler (Ernest Truex), convinced that the salesman can give him everything necessary to become successful. He snatches a pair of shoes from the old man's briefcase and slips into them, thinking that the shoes will carry him to a place that will bring him good fortune. He then gets hit by a car, closing out an undistinguished life.

The episode consists of three distinct segments: Nate's discovery of the footwear; his nearly-passionate encounter with Wilma, wife of the dead man; and the ever-so-brief encounter of Nate and the killers. They recognize the shoes and overhear his drink order ("tequila with a cube of sugar", changed from "tequila with lemon" in the script), which leads to Nate's quick demise and the cycle repeating once more. The flavor is that of a miniature film noir or perhaps even a scene from *Perry Mason*. Like a number of other *Zone* stories, including many of Serling's early episodes of the series, "Dead Man's Shoes" takes place entirely at night. As *The Twilight Zone* was a prime-time show, this allowed the audience to feel like they were witnessing the action as it was happening.

All this was projected well by its director, Montgomery Pittman, whose prowess extended beyond direction; he wrote three fine episodes of *The Twilight Zone*, which he also directed, starring such actors as Lee Marvin, James Best, Charles Bronson and Elizabeth Montgomery. His work on the series was a reflection of an enormous talent.

In the lead, Warren Stevens takes a deadpan approach to the part that works wonderfully well. Joan Marshall-Ashby adds just the right touch of hysteria as the voluptuous Wilma. No less convincing are character actors Richard Devon as Dagget and Ben Wright as a fellow derelict.

The Twilight Zone was sometimes railed on by critics for being a "thinking person's show," which required the audience to take an active part in the stories. "Dead Man's Shoes" was no exception to this rule. For instance, how does Nate Bledsoe undergo the quick metamorphosis from street man to suave gangster? What force leads him to the posh apartment where he knows the ins and outs surprisingly well? As Ritch has specified, the character is supposed to be "a wine-soaked bum who has to play a gangster role for which he is unsuited by temperament or manner." As directed and acted here, the transition between the two phases is more or less imperceptible and the audience has to draw conclusions of their own. The gangsters who see to Nate's demise seem to be ersatz mafia sharks but their occupation is never made clear. Also left to conjecture is how long this chain of events has persisted, and we can only guess as to the other dramatis personae who have been lucky, or unlucky, enough to be subject to the unique articles of attire.

"Dead Man's Shoes" was originally broadcast on 19 January, 1962.

DEAD MAN'S SHOES

<u>CAST</u>

NATE BLEDSOE   a wine-soaked bum, who has to play a Gangster role for which he is unsuited by temperament or manner

SAM   tough Bowery bum

CHIPS   cast-off Englishman of Skid Row

WILMA   lush physically; dense mentally

MAITRE D'

DAGGET'S WOMAN   a tart

DAGGET   late model gangster; you couldn't tell him from your insurance broker or banker

JIMMY   Dagget's slightly tougher companion

BEN   another Jimmy

<u>SETS</u>

EXT. SKID ROW – Alley, nearby bar, etc.

EXT. GOOD APARTMENT SECTION

INT. ORNATELY FURNISHED APT. – Living room, bedroom, shower room

INT. SMALL NIGHT CLUB

INT. NIGHT CLUB OFFICE AND CORRIDOR

THE TWILIGHT ZONE – "Dead Man's Shoes"
Rev. 9/28/61

FADE IN:

1. EXT STREET   WIDE ANGLE NIGHT

Slums. Deserted. Ominous. The sidewalks and street are damp from heavy fog. One eerie streetlight.

CAMERA HOLDS as a sedan rolls slowly INTO SCENE. It pauses, then turns into an alley.

2. INT ALLEY FULL SHOT   NIGHT

The auto stops near some ancient iron steps leading to the rear entrance of an ancient building. CAMERA FOCUSES ON rear door. A man gets out and looks up and down alley. The man is DAGGET.

                    DAGGET
    Okay. Dump him.

3-6. CAMERA MOVES PAST Dagget and we see the floor of the rear seat. A man is prone on it. A dapper young man comes around to grab the one on the floor by his shoulders. The body is dumped beneath the stairs. CAMERA PULLS BACK as the men get back in the car. The car pulls away. CAMERA HOLDS briefly on the body beneath the stairs. Then it RISES slowly to a landing on the old stairs.

Here we find another man (NATE). A bum, sleeping beneath old newspapers. He has witnessed the little drama below. With trembling fingers, he picks up a pint-sized wine bottle. No need to put it to his lips. He can tell it is empty. He drops it and gets to his feet. CAMERA FOLLOWS as he goes down the stairs, around the building, around the railing, and to the body. He kneels beside it.

7. CLOSE SHOT   NATE   BODY

He rifles the victim's pockets, working swiftly. His search discloses only one trifle: a key on an expensive looking chain. He pockets the key.

8. MED. SHOT

Nate regains an erect posture and is moving away when the shoes catch his eye.

9. HIS POV

The two-tones, shining in the lamplight, are the finest footgear Nate has seen in many years. The CAMERA PANS DOWN to his own feet. The shoes we see are hardly worthy of the name. Newspaper protrudes through a split between sole and upper of one, from the other a big toe extends itself freely. The leather is cracked and rotten.

10. MED CLOSE SHOT

Wasting little time, Nate squats beside the corpse and twists one of its feet to assay their size.

11. CLOSE SHOT

Nate transfers the new shoes to his own feet. He stands up, out of FRAME, tests the fit by stamping his feet. Apparently satisfied he takes a step or two away. THE CAMERA MOVES with his feet. He halts, then returns to the dead man. His HAND enters FRAME from above, picks up his discarded footgear. He walks a few feet down the alley, pauses. We HEAR the old shoes being thrown into a trash can. THE CAMERA CONTINUES TO MOVE with his feet as he retraces his steps past the corpse, out of the alley and onto the sidewalk. The new shoes click along the pavement. Nate's step is vigorous, healthy and purposeful.

12.   WHIP PAN TO:

13. SERLING

                SERLING
Nathan Edward Bledsoe, of the Bowery Bledsoes: a man, once—a spectre now, one of those myriad modern-day ghosts that haunt the reeky nights of the city, in search of a flop, a handout, a glass of forgetfulness.
       (beat)
Nate doesn't know it, but his search is about to end. because those shiny new shoes are going to carry him right into the capitol of The Twilight Zone.

FADE TO BLACK.

COMMERCIAL

FADE IN:

14. EXT STREET   CLOSE SHOT THE SHOES

Clicking along the sidewalk, seeming to have a life of their own.

15. EXT SKID ROW BUILDINGS   MOVING SHOT   NIGHT

Nate is walking at a brisk clip along skid row as neon lights blink rhythmically. His head is up, eyes forward. He seems to have shed several years since the donning of the new shoes. Two loungers, hunched in the doorway of a mission, turn their heads to follow him. One—a fat, rough-hewn bum named SAM—steps out and calls.

                SAM
      Hey, Nate!

Nate halts slowly, as though being awakened from a trance. He turns toward the two men.

16. MED SHOT   EXT ROCK OF AGES MISSION

A typical Bowery Mission: reconverted store. In b.g. we HEAR a hymn raggedly moaned by denizens of the neighborhood.

                NATE
        (hesitantly)
    Yeah, what d'ya want?

                SAM
    Nothin'...just wondered where you was goin'.
        (suggestively)
    Make a little strike?

                NATE
       (shaking his head)
Nah.
        (starts off)

                           SAM
                    So what's the hurry?

                           NATE
                    (genuinely confused)
                    I dunno.
                           (starts off again)

                           SAM
                    (taking his arm, threateningly)
                    Nate, don't kid a buddy. You're after a jug.

16. CONTINUED

Nate attempts to pull away, but Sam holds him tight. The other man steps from the doorway. This is CHIPS, a tall, faintly aristocratic Britisher in his sixties, gone almost entirely to seed.

                           CHIPS
                    (to Sam)
                    Sam! What's come over you?

With his fingertips he delivers a pugnacious poke against Sam's chest. He then turns and embraces Nate fraternally.

                           CHIPS
                    I see the whole thing. Clearly, this is a case of
                    assault and battery.

                           SAM
                    Whattya talkin'—I'm only—

                           CHIPS
                    (interrupting; to Nate)
                    I'd be happy to testify for you in a court action.

                           NATE
                    Aah, forget it. He didn't mean nothin'.

                    CHIPS
                (approvingly)
        Spoken like a gentleman...
                (to Sam)
        Now, you see? Aren't you ashamed?
        To think for a moment that such a man of honor
        would refuse to share a windfall with his comrades...

                    NATE
        I dunno what you're talkin' about.

                    CHIPS
        Now, now, Nathan...don't destroy the image I've
        created.
                (He looks significantly at the
                new shoes.)
        It's rather obvious ...you've struck something.
        We couldn't help noticing your...purposeful
        stride—your air of well being...
                (significantly)
        your new shoes. Quite expensive, aren't they?

                    NATE
        I found 'em...in an alley.

17. CLOSE SHOT   THE THREE PAIRS OF FEET

Nate's new brogans providing startling contrast. Nate's hand appears IN FRAME. He flicks away specks of dust from the shoetops with a grimy handkerchief.

                    CHIPS (O.S.)
        Looks like British workmanship to me.
        But aren't they a bit too snug?

                    NATE (O.S.)
                (straightening)
        Yeah, they do feel a little funny...

18. BACK TO SCENE

                    CHIPS
         I'd be happy to—

                    NATE
              (quickly interrupting)
         But they fit okay.

                    CHIPS
         Yes. Uh, Nathan…when you found the footgear,
         did you also by any remote chance, run across…

Nate suddenly becomes hard.

                    NATE
         Just the shoes.

Nate moves to a window to study his reflection in it. It's like he is seeing a stranger. Tentatively, he touches his cheek.

Sam and Chips exchange glances at this unusual expression. Suddenly, Nate whirls and starts away. Quickly, Sam puts an arm out and grasps his shoulder.

                    SAM
         Now where are you headed for, Pal?

Nate looks at Sam. No longer the look of a frightened wino. But the look of an assured and somehow evil person. He speaks quietly.

                    NATE
         Take your hand off me.

Now it is Sam who feels the cold chill. He removes his hand. Sam and Chips watch as Nate swings off down the street, walking with the air of a man who has somewhere to go and is going there.

DISSOLVE TO:

20. CONTINUED

                    SAM
         See, what'd I tell you? He's onto somethin', awright.

                    CHIPS
                (thoughtfully)
            Or something is on to him...
                (he shudders)
            Good Sam, when a denizen of this particular
            jungle snubs the equivalent of a drink and a
            flop, it may be surmised that he is in the grip of
            strange and unnatural forces...

                    SAM
                (nodding)
            Yeah, you can say that again.

DISSOLVE TO:

21. CLOSE SHOT   MOVING

We follow Nate's feet and legs as he walks. He has left Skid Row as evidenced by the character of the sidewalk and type of store fronts we can see in B.G.

22. CLOSE SHOT   MOVING

The sidewalk is now broad and smooth. Occasionally the shoes traverse insets of marble or patterned concrete common to upper bracket shopping districts.

23. WIDER ANGLE

The B.G. here is a swanky apartment building. We follow Nate's feet along past the polished brass hydrants and bronze plaque of THE MAYFAIR apartments. THE CAMERA HOLDS on the plaque and Nate walks out of FRAME.

24. MED SHOT

He stands under the canopy over the entrance to the building, looks toward the door in B.G., takes a step forward and pauses.

25. CLOSE SHOT

Nate twists his head from side to side. A completely baffled look distorts his features. He is bewildered at being in this strange location. Then, as though seized by an external force, he moves into the entrance.

DISSOLVE TO:

26. INT APARTMENT BUILDING HALL   NIGHT

The door to Apartment 621.

The CAMERA HOLDS on the door as Nate enters FRAME. He stops, looks at the number, fumbles in his pocket, brings out the key, looks at it dully. Thrusting it in the lock, he flings the door open.

27. HIS POV

The apartment is a tribute to bad taste and the money to indulge it. As garishly modern as a Las Vegas slot machine, the front room is brilliantly lit, over-furnished. A couch present sits back to us. Facing it are two sectionals, arranged in a "conversational" group. Cocktail table between, false fireplace to the left. In B.G. there is a chrome-and-ebony bar, laden with specialized drinking equipment and a TV set. A GIRL (WILMA) is lying on her back on the thick pile white carpet. Before her television screen flickers ineffectually. One of her legs is extended up the back of the sectional couch, the other crossed at the knee as he paints her toenails. The sound of the lock's tumblers distracts her and she twists around.

28. LOW ANGLE PAST GIRL

From this angle all we can see is the pair of shoes.

>   WILMA
>   (surprised, relieved, happy)
>   Dane! I'm so glad...

29. MED SHOT NATE – HER POV

She breaks off as she realizes that the man is not Dane. Nate closes the door, as he stares at her.

30. MED SHOT WILMA – NATE'S POV

She springs to her feet, backs against the facing sectionals. Lush, bosomy, dressed in skin-tight velvet Capri pants and a scoop-necked sweater, she matches the apartment perfectly.

31. CLOSE SHOT

                    WILMA
               (tautly)
          Who *are you?*
               (beat)
          What do you want?

32. ANOTHER ANGLE TO INCLUDE NATE

Nate does not reply but moves directly into the room. Wilma watches his progress in alarm. CAMERA FOLLOWS NATE.

CONTINUED

                    WILMA
               (frightened and threatening)
          You'd better get out of here…

He continues to ignore her and threads his way though the furniture barriers to the bar, pours a big wallop of tequila and downs it. He stands for a moment, then heaves a sigh of satisfaction.

                    WILMA
          That's Dane's bottle. If Dane comes back and finds
          you here, he'll kill you.

Nate turns around slowly and studies the girl. His face is different now. Very different. In subtle ways it has become a strong, almost cruel face.

                    NATE
          That's why I'm drinking from it.

                    WILMA
          Y'hear what I'm…saying…
               (something in Nate's expression
               causes her to falter)
          He'll…kill…you.

Nate walks toward the girl. She takes a backward step. He is next to her now. Slowly he lifts his hand and touches her cheek. Then he turns and starts for the bedroom. Wilma recovers herself, makes a lunge at the front door.

                          NATE
         Wilma!

His voice is utterly different: imperative, threatening. The girl freezes.

                       NATE (CONT'D)
                    Fix me a drink.

He goes to the bedroom door, opens it, walks in, closes it again. The girl stands very still for a long moment, then starts for the front door.

                     NATE'S VOICE (O.S.)
                 You'd never make it downstairs.

Appalled and confused, she stares off at the closed bedroom door.

33. INT BEDROOM   FULL SHOT

In keeping with the rest of the apartment, there is a low ben, another TV set, modern lamps, a huge chest of drawers and a walk-in closet whose open door discloses a long-rack of pin-striped suits and loud patterned sports jackets. Almost without seeing, Nate strides to the chest, whips open a drawer, extracts an automatic and tosses it on the bed. Then, taking shirt, shorts and socks in one motion, he moves to the closet and grabs a suit off the rack. Carrying the clothing with him, he steps into the adjacent bathroom and clothing with him, he steps into the adjacent bathroom and closes the door. We presently HEAR a shower turned on.

34. INT BATHROOM MED SHOT

Nate strips off the filthy coat and shirt he is wearing, stuffing them down the laundry chute in a distasteful manner. THE CAMERA MOVES IN to a CLOSE SHOT of Nate's upper body as he removes his trousers. He steps before the mirror, picks up an electric razor plugged in there begins to shave.

35. FRONT ROOM   MED SHOT

Wilma is listening outside the bedroom door to the sounds from the bathroom which filter through the thin walls of the apartment. She turns to the telephone which is placed on a low table and dials a number. When it answers, she speaks anxiously into the mouthpiece.

> WILMA
> Bernie? Wilma. Is Dane there?

Her face falls at the unheard answer.

> WILMA (CONT'D)
> Oh? Well, if the comes back, tell him...
> (helplessly)
> Tell him...I need him, right away. I'm at the apartment.

36. CLOSE SHOT   NATE'S FEET

Nate steps to the shower door and slips out of the shoes and automatically steps into the shower.

37. CLOSE SHOT   NATE

Nate stands in the shower with the water running over him. He is dazed and stares about in uncomprehending fashion. He rubs his hands over his face as though trying to determine who he is. A look of fear comes to his eyes and he bolts out of the shower. THE CAMERA PULLS BACK WITH HIM as he blots himself hastily with a towel.

38. ANOTHER ANGLE

Nate catches sight of himself in the mirror and is dumbfounded at his clean-shaven appearance, and his unaccustomed nudity. He looks wildly about for his apparel. Not seeing his familiar clothing, he snatches at the garments hanging on the door and begins to dress.

39. INT BEDROOM   FULL SHOT

The door opens. Wilma cautiously pokes her head through the door, then steps inside. She sees the gun lying on the bed and moves quickly toward it.

40. MED CLOSE SHOT

Picking up the gun in an unfamiliar manner, the girl aims it tentatively toward the bathroom door. She starts in surprise but maintains her threatening pose as a CLICK from the latch announces that Nate is coming out.

                    WILMA
             All right, mister.

41. ANGLE PAST WILMA

Nate stands just ouside the bathroom clumsily dressed except for the shoes which he carries in one hand. He stares blankly and fearfully at the girl and the gun.

                    WILMA
             Where's Dane?

Nate looks at her. Rubs his forehead.

                    NATE
                (blankly)
             Dane? I'm sorry...I don't...understand.

                    WILMA
                (angrily)
             Oh, yes you do!
                (motioning)
             You've got his shoes. Nobody else wears
             shoes like Dane's!

42. POV

He peers at the shoes in his hand.

43. PREVIOUS ANGLE

                    NATE
             I don't know what you're talking about. Honest!
                (beat)
             I found the shoes...
                (trying to remember)

                    WILMA
             You mean you *stole* them.

Nate recognizes the threat of the gun and makes haste to agree with her.

NATE
Yeah…that's right…I stole them.

WILMA
Where?

NATE
Miss, please—I don't know anything about it. I—

WILMA
(cutting in)
At the Club?

NATE
What?

WILMA
What was he doing there?

NATE
(pitifully)
I don't know!

WILMA
What *do* you know, Mister?

NATE
Nothing.

There is such simple and profound conviction in that one word that the girl yields to unaccustomed pity.

WILMA
I oughtta kill you, bustin' in here like this, like you owned the place…

NATE
(whining)
Please, don't do that.

43. CONTINUED

                    WILMA
        All right. But you get outta here…now!

                    NATE
        Yes, Miss…yes…I'll go.

44. CLOSE SHOT

Nate sits down on the bed and draws on the shoes. When he raises his head to face Wilma again, he has become the same hard, terse character as before. He stares at the girl with narrowed eyes.

45. MED SHOT

Taking two steps forward, Nate wrests the gun angrily away from Wilma, as though taking a dangerous toy from a child.

                    NATE
        I thought I told you to fix me a drink.

                    WILMA
                 (terrified)
        Look, Mister…

                    NATE
                 (in amazement)
        What do I have to do, break your arm?

                    WILMA
                 (placatingly)
        Okay…okay…

46. APARTMENT FULL SHOT   FRONT ROOM

The girl moves to the ebony bar and stands by it indecisively. Nate emerges from the bedroom. He is in the act of putting the gun into an armpit holster. As he reaches the bar, he knows a tie swiftly. Wilma has not made a move to fix the drink, so he taps on the counter top.

                                    NATE
                             The drink!

                                    WILMA
                                 (frightened)
                             What'll it be?

CONTINUED

                                    NATE
                        'What'll it be...' What do I always have?

                                    WILMA
                        I don't know. Honest, Mister, I don't know!
                                    (beat)

47. TWO SHOT

                                    NATE
                                  (angrily)
                             Tequila...with lemon.

She looks around for the decanter. He thrusts it at her. The lip of the bottle tinkles against the glass as she shakes. Squeezing a half lemon over the drink, she hands it to Nate who has been admiring her lush fullness.

                                    WILMA
                             Who *are* you?

                                    NATE
                             You tell *me*.

He moves close to the girl. She shrinks back.

                                    WILMA
                        Dane's due any second. I'm warnin' you. If you
                        know what's good for you...

                                    NATE
                                  (smiling)
                        I know what's good for me. You.

She breaks for the door. He catches her, making a prison of his arms. She struggles; he reaches out, flips off the light.

                    WILMA
          Don't touch me...don't—

Suddenly Nate kisses her, a long embrace mixing brutality and passion. The girl's struggles cease.

                    NATE
                  (softly)
          Who am I, baby?

                    WILMA
                  (a whisper)
          Dane!

CONTINUED

47. CONTINUED

He kisses her again. She yields a long moment, then reaches for the light switch. The lights flash on.

                    WILMA
                  (hysterical)
          No, you're not Dane! You're not! You're not!

                    NATE
          Be quiet!

                    WILMA
                  (shrieking)
          What have you done with him? What's happened?
          What's happened—

Nate slaps her, hard. It breaks the hysteria. Sobbing, the girl sinks to the floor.

48. LOW ANGLE

Nate stands by the fallen girl for a moment, then moves away toward the front door. She hesitates, then calls to him.

                             WILMA
                 Wait…

Nate's stride does not break. When he reaches the door, he turns around.

                              NATE
                 I've got a little unfinished business…where's
                 Bernie Dagget.

He bends down INTO FRAME and flicks a speck a speck of dust from the shoes with his handkerchief.

                             WILMA
                 At the club.

                              NATE
                 But I'll be back. You wait here.

THE CAMERA CLOSES IN FOR A TIGHT SHOT OF THE SHOES. The door opens, the shoes step through and the door closes as we

                                            FADE TO BLACK

49. INT APEX CLUB   FULL SHOT

A bar of some elegance or a very small supper club according to how you look at it. A pianist plays somewhere.

50. INT VESTIBULE   MED SHOT

As above patter goes on, Nate scans the room.

51. LONG SHOT   TABLE NATE'S POV

Nearby, a group of people are gathered at a small table. The men are criminals, the women their molls; but styles in the underworld change, too. These men are well-dressed, impeccably turned out, quiet in manner. They could be businessmen. Their women are expensive-looking and beautiful but not dumb flappers. BERNARD DAGGET, a pleasant, pink-cheeked, cologne-scented man in his late forties, is in a celebration mood, champagne glass extended. He is the man we saw at the shooting, scene #1.

52. BACK TO NATE   IN VESTIBULE

The maitre d' comes forward.

                    MAITRE D'
          Yes, sir?

                    NATE
          I'd like a table.

                    MAITRE D'
          You have a reservation?

                    NATE
              (ignoring this; pointing o.s.)
          That one over there, next to Dagget.

                    MAITRE D'
              (rather coldly)
          I am afraid that table is reserved. If you would
          care to wait at the bar, perhaps—

Very casually, Nate pulls out the roll of bills and skins off three tens. In doing so, he never takes his eyes from the Dagget group, o.s.

                    NATE
              (pressing the bills into maitre d's hand)
          Let's go, Ferdie.

                    MAITRE D'
          Yes, sir. Thank you, sir.
              (grins)
          I should have known you would have a reservation.

53. FULL SHOT   CLUB FLOOR

The maitre d' leads Nate across the room.

54. DAGGET TABLE   MED SHOT

Dagget laughs boisterously at someone's joke. As Nate pauses by the table, Dagget flicks a glance toward him. It is not significant. He sees only a new customer.

55. ANGLE TO NATE

Smiling at Dagget, he continues behind the maitre d' to the opposite table. Before he sits down he raises a shoe to the chair, dabs at it, then at the other, with a handkerchief, in the characteristic mannerism. The maitre d' notices. Nate seats himself.

> MAITRE D'
> What may I bring you, sir?

> NATE
> Tequila. With lemon.

> MAITRE D'
> (reacting)
> Yes, sir.

Very relaxed, Nate lights a cigarette, settles back and grins in the direction of Dagget.

56. DAGGET'S TABLE

Dagget's eyes are drawn from the stage to the opposite table, o.s. A slight cloud of apprehension passes over his eyes. Then he looks back to his companions. But again his eyes are drawn to

57. NATE

who is staring at him, smiling his broad, somehow evil and promising smile. It contains little mirth.

58. NATE'S TABLE   CLOSE

Never taking his eyes off Dagget, he applauds warmly. A waiter serves his drink.

59. DAGGET'S TABLE   CLOSE

He and his friends. Dagget looks over again in Nate's direction.

60. NATE   CLOSE

He raises the glass to Dagget in a toast.

61. BACK TO DAGGET

Peering at Nate. His woman notices.

                    DAGGET'S WOMAN
        Friend of yours?

Dagget shakes his head, then leans over to one of his male companions, a burly young man with small, cold eyes.

                    DAGGET
        Jimmy, that fella over there...you know him?

Jimmy's eyes lash up and back.

                    JIMMY
        Negative.

                    DAGGET
        What about you, Ben?

The paunchy, middle-aged man named Ben repeats Jimmy's action.

                    BEN
        I've never seen him before in my life. Why?

                    DAGGET
        Well, he seems to know *us*.

                    JIMMY
        A lush. Forget it.

                  DAGGET'S WOMAN
        What makes you think he's looking at *you* anyway?
        Or don't you think I'm worth staring at any more?

                    DAGGET
            (looking in direction of Nate)
        What?

                  DAGGET'S WOMAN
        Oh, nothing...I just said I was leaving you.

                    DAGGET
            (trying for his old humor)
        There's only one way people leave me, honey.
        Feet first.

He tries to put Nate out of his mind. Settles back, turns the chair. But it's no good. As though feeling the heat of Nate's eyes on the back of his neck, he whirls around.

62. HIS POV

The grin never wavering, the eyes staring unblinkingly.

63. BACK TO DAGGET TABLE

                    DAGGET'S WOMAN
        Look, you're driving me crazy. Why don't you
        get rid of the guy, or invite him over, or *something*!

Dagget thinks it over. He nods at Ben, who rises and starts for

64. NATE'S TABLE

Ben walks up to Nate, who doesn't indicate awareness of the man's presence.

                    BEN
        Hey.

Nate looks up, slowly.

                    NATE
        You talking to me?

                    BEN
        Dagget wants you. Over there.

                    NATE
        An invitation to join Bernie Dagget at his own
        personal table? I don't know what to say.

                    BEN
        Don't say nothing. Just do it.

                        NATE
            All right. I accept.

They move out. Ben carries Nate's chair.

65. DAGGET'S TABLE

Ben puts the chair down beside Dagget.

                        NATE
            Hello, Bernie.

                        DAGGET
            You know me?

                        NATE
                (nodding)
            By reputation.

                        DAGGET
            Oh.
                (decides it's flattery)
            Oh, I get it. Sit down.

                        NATE
            Thanks. You celebrating something?

He seats himself. A waiter appears.

                        DAGGET
            Yes. What are you drinkin'?

                        NATE
            Tequila. With lemon.

Dagget and the others react to this.

                        NATE
            If that's okay…

                        DAGGET
            Sure. It's just…kind of a funny coincidence.

NATE
Oh? How's that?

DAGGET
I had a good friend who drank the same stuff.

Nate nods and goes on smiling his mirthless, knowing smile.

DAGGET
What's your name?

NATE
Kilroy.

JIMMY
Look, buddy, when Mr. Dagget asks you—
(Dagget silences him with a wave)

DAGGET
What's your business?

NATE
Well, you might call me a messenger.
(beat)
I've got a message for *you*, Mr. Dagget.

DAGGET
Yeah? Well, let's have it.

CONTINUED

NATE
(shaking his head)
No. I was given instructions to deliver this message privately. It's kind of a touchy matter. You understand.

DAGGET
Who's it from?

NATE
(accepting drink from waiter)
I'm afraid I can't say.

He sips at the drink, then sets it down and smiles at the people.

NATE
(nodding toward o.s. stage)
This is a nice place. Real nice.

He sits sideways on the chair and flicks at his shoes.

66. CLOSE SHOT DAGGET

Looking at the shoes, then up at Nate again.

67. NEW ANGLE   ON TABLE

DAGGET
What'd the guy look like…that gave you the message?

NATE
Mr. Dagget, my business is forgetting, not remembering.

DAGGET
All right, messenger. Let's go.
(rises)
You girls wait here. We'll be back in a minute.

Jimmy and Ben rise.

NATE
(shakes his head)
It's got to be private.

DAGGET
It will be.

They walk away from the table.

68. VESTIBULE

The men walk into the dark alcove. Dagget leads the way to a door. He opens it with a key.

69. INT OFFICE   MED SHOT

An attractive room in the modern style: while rug, colorful sectional, abstract paintings, a kidney-shaped desk. The men enter.

>   NATE
> Very nice.
>   (taps wall)
> Sound-proofed too. That's smart.

70. GROUP SHOT

As the door closes, Jimmy starts to frisk Nate. He finds the shoulder holster at once, plucks out the gun, pockets it and steps back.

>   DAGGET
> You *still* got a message for me?

>   NATE
> Yes. And tell your monkey I want my gun back afterwards.

Dagget nods and motions to his boys, who exit the room.

71. NEW ANGLE

Nate smiles, locks the door, walks to the desk, sits down and props up his feet.

>   NATE
> Well, Bernie. Bernie...Bernie...
>   (glancing at center of floor)
> How'd ya get it cleaned so fast?

>   DAGGET
> What?

                    NATE
        The rug. Blood's pretty hard to get out, isn't it?

                    DAGGET
        I don't know what you're talkin' about.

CONTINUED

71. CONTINUED

                    NATE
        Then you know what I'll do, Bernie? I'll *tell* him
        what I'm talking about. I'm talking about a guy
        who had a nice thing going for him...plenty of
        dough, plenty of action...only he wasn't happy
        because he had a partner. That meant he couldn't
        be number one, see. And being number one was
        very important to him. So he offered to buy the
        partner out. And when the partner refused to
        sell...he killed him.
                (pointing)
        Right there it happened. And you'd never guess.
        It was a slick job.

                    DAGGET
                (beginning to tremble)
        Who are you?

                    NATE
        I told you. A messenger.
                (face turns hard)
        And here's the message.

72. CLOSE ON NATE

He swivels in the chair and fires three shots at the oil painting.

73. CLOSE ON OIL PAINTING

The bullet-riddled body of Jimmy comes ripping through the thin canvas.

74. CLOSE ON NATE

...turning quickly back to Dagget.

> NATE
> You didn't think it'd work twice, did you?

75. CLOSE ON DAGGET

His eyes wide.

> DAGGET
> (choking out the word)
> Dane!

76. NEW ANGLE   NATE FAVORED

Almost leisurely, he pulls back the hammer of the gun and prepares to squeeze the trigger. A single shot rings out. Nate drops his gun, clutches at his chest, looks off toward Ben who is stepping into the room through a door formed by the full-length mirror. The mirror, of the two-way variety – is shattered, Ben's having shot directly through it.

77. FAVORING NATE

...who tumbles out of the chair, onto the rug.

78. BIG CLOSEUP   NATE

> NATE
> (choked whisper)
> I'll be back, Bernie...I'll keep coming back...
> again and again...and I'll get you. So help me,
> I'll get you...

79. TWO SHOT   DAGGET AND BEN

> BEN
> Who is he?

> DAGGET
> I don't know. I don't know. I do know.

They look at each other, as we

DISSOLVE TO:

80. EXT SKID ROW   MED SHOT   NIGHT

Chips EXITS a tavern rather peremptorily, as Nate had done in the opening shots. Recovering his dignity, he shouts:

> CHIPS
> You'll hear from my attorneys!!

Chips staggers off, toward CAMERA. He is obviously high, whether on booze or ether fumes, we know not. He rummages through his pockets, finds a butt, studies its stunted remains, tosses it sadly aside and stumbles forth into the night.

81.   ANGLE ON CHIPS

He weaves uncertainly by a dark and reeking alley. He pauses.

82. MED CLOSE SHOT   BODY OF NATE

Hidden by darkness, only the shoes showing. Chips hurries INTO FRAME. He reacts with a little drunken cry of alarm at the sight of Nate, starts off. Then, noticing the shoes, pauses again.

83.   NEW ANGLE

Chips looks at his own poor shoes, which are in leathery ribbons; then, quickly, he removes the fancy brogans and forces his feet into them.

> CHIPS
> Forgive me, Nathan…but you'll have no use for these now.
>   (beat; walks around in shoes as a customer
>   in a shoe store might test a purchase)
> Perfect!

84.   NEW ANGLE ON CHIPS

He passes a refuse cage, and, smiling, drops his filthy shoes into it.

85. TRAVELING SHOT   ON SHOES

They tap along the pavement at an ever-increasing rate, the tread becoming more and more determined. As they turn a corner, and tap-tap-tap their way to darkness, we hear

> SERLING'S VOICE (O.S.)
> There's an old saying that goes…
> "If the shoe fits, wear it." But be careful.
> If you happen to find a pair of size 9 black-and-white loafers, with perforated uppers and silver buckles…made to order in the old country…
> be very careful. You might walk right into
> The Twilight Zone.

FADE OUT

THE END

JOHN FURIA, Jr.
"I Dream of Genie"

Without a sponsor in tow for the coming fall, *The Twilight Zone* was cancelled in the spring of 1962 after three groundbreaking seasons. However, the cancellation was rescinded when a sub-par hour-length program had to be replaced. Things got back in gear and eighteen episodes were produced between the fall of 1962 and the spring of 1963. Prior to the cancellation, CBS had considered converting *The Twilight Zone* into an hour show. With thirty additional minutes, more drama could be offered. But for a series that had succeeded in a short time block, more drama did not necessarily mean better drama. The writers found that material often had to be added just to fill the time. Says one writer of early television, "For a typical season of approximately thirty episodes, you're going to have about five great ones, another twenty that run the gamut of average, and another five that, for whatever reason, don't really work as well as they should." While more than several of these hour segments succeeded greatly, most of those remaining read well but would have fared better in the old half-hour format. "I Dream of Genie" by John Furia, Jr. falls into this category.

Serling's earlier episode "The Man in the Bottle" showed an older couple visited by a genie who grants them four wishes. They end up no worse for the wear, and no better. Furia's script is fleshed out quite a bit, but is much the same—the main difference being that the focal character, office worker George P. Hanley, gets a chance to move up in the world—rather, move up and 'out' of it—and himself become a genie. Similar to Serling's "No Time Like the Past," a time travel story produced the same season, the main character visits four distinct tableauxes of life in attempt to alter the present.

In the starring role as George P. Hanley was comedian and later comedy director Howard Morris, who had recently appeared alongside Sid Caesar in *Your Show of Shows* and *Caesar's Hour*. Around the same time as this appearance on *The Twilight Zone* he was also making guest appearances on *The Andy Griffith Show* as laughably annoying mountain man Ernest T. Bass. Morris replaced a less competent actor originally cast in the part. However, he was hampered by a dullard character that was far from comedic. Despite success with a few brighter moments, including a scene where George flirts with a young lady underneath a piano at a lavish party, the humor often emerges flaccidly and the sight gags fail to impress. Tying the threads of each scene together are short sequences featuring a Scottish terrier named Atilla, a plot device presumably used to keep the story moving along. Additionally, the director did not stress fast-paced dramatic progression, and this is perhaps what made the story suffer. But comedy was never a forte of the series. Serling and others tried their hands at the more light-hearted form sporadically over five seasons, and the results were usually interesting but not spectacular.

This is not to say that the episode's writer suffered from incompetence. John Furia remains a respected figure in the television writing community and academia. He wrote episodes of *The Chrysler Theater, The Waltons, The Dirty Dozen*, and *Kung Fu*, as well as the pilot for the long running series *Hotel*. For many years, he served as president of the Writers Guild of America. He is also the founding chairman and Professor of the Division of Writing at the renowned School of Cinema-Television at the University of Southern California. Furia also wrote a number of Movies of the Week and nearly one-hundred dramas for the public service series *Insight*, which Rod Serling also wrote for. The award-winning film "We Are the Children," starring Ted Danson and Ally Sheedy, was written by him. He also produced two mini-series', "Rage of Angels" and Hemingway's "The Sun Also Rises," for NBC.

Of "I Dream of Genie," Furia says, "I was asked to write a script for *The Twilight Zone* by its then producer, Herb Hirschman, with whom I'd had a fruitful relationship on other series he had produced. My first reaction was that I was not comfortable with a science fiction approach which some of the shows had, but that I very much enjoyed the unpredictable stories of men and women who found themselves in unusual if not one-of-a-kind circumstances and how their lives were changed. The story idea popped into my head one evening. What if a man came across a magic lamp and had to choose what wish to make? We all dream of such a situation so I believed there was a universal theme in my idea. I played with it until I had worked out the details and pitched it to Herb Hirschman who approved it and I wrote the script without many of the frustrations that frequently hover around the edges of an initial idea. I changed very little of it as I went and did not have to do much in the usual second draft. I also had the temerity to write Serling's introduction for the story, attempting to capture his signature off beat humor and tone. It pleased me greatly that he used my intro word for word. My family liked the episode more than I did. I had imagined a Genie more like a Madison Avenue huckster, but it was played with an effete style that made the piece in my mind less Puckish and not as amusing. Nevertheless I thought it was a pleasing *Twilight Zone* and one that had something to say as all the better ones did."

"I Dream of Genie" was originally broadcast on 21 March, 1963.

I DREAM OF GENIE

(Working Title: "Do Unto Others")

FADE IN:

1. INT GIFT SHOT ANGLE ON SHIPPING CRATE DAY

Streamers of excelsior reach like tentacles over the wooden sides, as a young, nattily dressed CLERK bends over the crate to extract more of its contents. He pulls out several small cut-glass perfume bottles, and sets them out on a table.

                    CLERK
Three glass perfume bottles…

2. ANGLE TO INCLUDE THE PROPRIETOR

An elegantly dressed salesman in a world of salesmen, he winces at his clerk's lack of sensitivity.

                    SALESMAN
         (writing on his pad; an
         inventory)
Three crystal bottles…to imprison the…attar of damask rose petals…

                    CLERK
         (reacts, takes out ceramic jugs)
Pottery jugs…two.

                    SALESMAN
"Pottery jugs!" Where's your aesthetic sense? You can't entice anyone to buy "pottery jugs"!

                    CLERK
You really think people buy somethin' 'cause of what you call it?

                    SALESMAN
              (sagely)
     People don't *buy* anything in a gift shop: they
     come because they don't know *what* they want.
     Then *I sell* them something!

                    CLERK
     So, whattaya call the pottery jugs?

                    SALESMAN
              (speculates a moment, then
              rhapsodic)
     We'll display them alongside a couple of those
     silk pillows…with a loaf of dark bread, "A loaf of
     bread, a jug of wine, and thou beside me singing
     in the wilderness…"
              (gleefully)
     I'll unload them in three days!

3.   ANGLE ON CLERK

He reacts, then dives down to search in the recesses of the crate for any leftovers. He comes up frowning and holding out a tarnished, battered, old oil lamp with a heavy base and a large bowl.

                    CLERK
     Okay, Omar, what about this?

4.   TWO SHOT

The salesman frowns, then shrugs.

                    SALESMAN
     When we buy a shipment from Morocco sight
     unseen, we take what we get!
              (ruefully)
     To sell *that*…I'll have to high pressure some
     unsuspecting, dumb sucker!

5.   INT GIFT SHOP ANGLE ON ENTRANCE

As George Hanley enters; a warm, timid man, about thirty, with a manner that would make a shy mouse seem arrogant. Even his hair refuses to be subservient to a comb. He hesitates at the entrance, looking about the gift shop dubiously.

>SALESMAN (O.C.)
>May I help you?

6. ANGLE SALESMAN & GEORGE

>GEORGE
>(hesitant)
>I hope so…I mean, I don't know. I'm not sure what I want.

>SALESMAN
>(recognizing a customer when
>he sees one)
>Suppose you tell me the occasion, and who it's intended for…and leave it to me?

The salesman takes his arm and gently steers him past a counter displaying assorted items: an elegant silver tea service, a voodoo mask, the perfume bottles, a manikin clothed in sheer silk "harem girl" pajamas which fail to conceal its imitation, plastic charms.

>GEORGE
>(fumbling)
>It has to be something…*very* special!

>SALESMAN
>A personal gift, sir?

>GEORGE
>(an embarrassed glance at the
>manikin)
>Not too personal. This girl in my office…she's like a goddess…I wouldn't want her to think that I was implying…that I was suggesting an intimacy between us that…I mean, I'd like it to be personal, but we're not. Yet….

He breaks off a tangle of embarrassment and confusion.

SALESMAN
(mentally already punching
up the sale)
I understand, sir.

The salesman swings into his act, advancing toward one object, then another, and obviously rejecting his first, inadequate thoughts. George follows him, pausing when he does, watching an artist giving the impression he is about to undertake the redecorating of the Sistine Chapel.

SALESMAN
(musing)
For a beautiful young lady...something truly *special*...Ah! I have it! I have it! Something for her desk!

George looks dubious.

GEORGE
She's got a big typewriter and a lot of pencils and...

SALESMAN
(overlapping)
Something to remind her of you through the trying moments of each day...subliminal... unique, but not bizarre...
(a sudden thought)
A hundred dollars would be too extravagant?...

George blanches, looks quickly for the exit.

GEORGE
A hundred dollars?

Overlapping, the salesman continues, moving across the floor to the rear, George following with growing trepidation. The man is a master. After a hundred dollars, anything is going to sound good.

SALESMAN
Of course. All wrong. She mustn't feel bought, but...romanced...
(claps his hands in ecstasy)

>   I have it! Perfect! Of course! Marvelous!

George reacts, his tongue almost hanging out at this display of enthusiasm. He follows the salesman to the low table in back where he reaches for something.

>   SALESMAN
>   It's ideal. It's romantic: not forward, yet...
>   "entime"...in a subtle way, of course. Voila!

He whirls around holding the beat-up lamp like a tiara on a velvet pillow. George stares.

>   GEORGE
>   That old...

>   SALESMAN
>   (overlapping)
>   This magnificent, old antique! A truly distinguished
>   antique—fit for a goddess!

Starts toward the cash register.

>   SALESMAN (CONT'D)
>   A perpetual reminder of your affection, your taste,
>   your individuality, your flair for romance! Fill this
>   with fresh flowers and she won't be able to pluck
>   you from her thoughts between nine and five...
>   after five, is up to you, sir! One of a kind, too;
>   note the tarnished metal; testifies to its authenticity...
>   and only twenty dollars!
>   (to clerk at the cash register)
>   Put this in a gift box for a most discriminating
>   gentleman.

Through this steamroller, George has been trapped between trying to inspect the lamp, and attempting to interrupt the gush of praise, with equal lack of success. Now the purchase seems complete before he can even get in his first word. He opens his mouth.

>   SALESMAN (CONT'D)
>   (shakes his hand)
>   Thank you, sir. And I hope you will allow me to

> serve you again...
> (a wink)
> When it's time for the engagement present!

Bulldozed, and half-believing, George has the pre-prepared box thrust in his hands, and turns over the money.

> SERLING (OVER)
> Meet Mr. George P. Hanley, a man life treats without deference, honor or success; waiters serve his soup cold; elevator operators close doors in his face; mothers never bother to wait up for the daughters he dates. George is a creature of humble habits and tame dreams; a square peg in a square rut...and by most recent definition, "an unsuspecting, dumb sucker."

George turns to leave the store, and the clerk shakes his head in disbelief, then offers his hand to his boss in resigned congratulations.

> DISSOLVE TO:

7. SERLING IN LIMBO SET

> SERLING
> He's an ordinary man, Mr. Hanley, but at this moment, the accidental possessor of a very special gift; the kind of gift that measures men against their dreams. The kind of gift most of us might ask for first, and possibly regret to the last, if we, like Mr. George P. Hanley, were about to plunge head-first and unaware into our own, personal Twilight Zone

> FADE TO BLACK.

> ACT I

FADE IN:

8. INT ACCOUNTING DEPT WATSON SAVINGS & LOAN DAY

Several precisely ordered rows of desks; a secretary's desk guards the walnut door to the boss's sanctuary at one end of the room. It is vacant for the moment; all the human digits in this number factory are out to lunch. Then CAMERA MOVES TO ADMIT George as he enters the room, bearing his gift package. George notes that he is alone, then with shy anticipation, sets his gift down on the secretary's desk. He admires it, somewhat dubiously, trying to picture how the box's hidden contents will look, as he rearranges its position. Hearing the approach of his fellows from the hall, he whisks the gift out of sight in the bottom drawer of his own desk, just as assorted co-workers enter, led by an aggressive, young bookkeeper, made more obnoxious by sleek good looks, ROGER HACKETT.

9. ANGLE ON GEORGE & ROGER

As Roger approaches his desk, adjacent to George's.

ROGER
(heartily)
Hey, Georgie Porgie. Where were you for lunch?

GEORGE
(winces at the nick-name)
I had some errands...

ROGER
(taps his belly)
You missed the world's champion worst chili con carne ever offered for human consumption. It set an historic new low, even for that greasy spoon Nick dares to call a diner.

GEORGE
I don't care much for chili.

ROGER
(settling at his desk)
Georgie, witness a solemn vow for me, willya?

GEORGE
(so square, he's a cube)
Right now? I'm afraid I have to enter these municipal bonds...

                    ROGER
                (overlaps)
        I, Roger Hackett, do solemnly swear, never again
        to commit gastronomic "hari-kari" at Nick's…
        beginning with the first day of my promotion
        to head bookkeeper…

This last is intended to get a rise out of George. It does.

                    GEORGE
        Your promotion?

                    ROGER
                (innocently)
        Sure.

                    GEORGE
        I thought Mr. Watson said each of us with equal
        seniority has an equal chance.

                    ROGER
                (enjoying the needling)
        That's correct, Georgie old Porgie! We're all
        equal…but some of us are just a teensy bit *more*
        equal than others! Especially *me*!

10.   ANGLE ON HALL DOORWAY

As ANN LAWSON, the boss' dazzling secretary, and the object of George's affection, enters. Miss Lawson would be a distraction anywhere; here she is the cause of retallying more figures than all the double-check procedures of the cost analysts. She hesitates an instant just inside the door, instinctively accentuating her presence in the room as effectively as if she blew a fanfare on Gabriel's trumpet.

11.   BACK TO ROGER AND GEORGE

Roger is staring in the direction of Miss Lawson, O.C., while George earnestly states his case.

                    GEORGE
        Mr. Watson is fair, Roger. Don't be overconfident.

I'm sure he'll weigh carefully our experience in
handling debit financing, and in evaluating liabilities...

      ROGER
    (reaching into his desk; overlaps)
That, old Georgie, is one reason why I am *more*
equal than you.

      GEORGE
What is?

Roger pulls from his desk a flat box, carefully gift-wrapped, and starts toward Miss Lawson as he finishes ticking off George.

      ROGER
All you think of is debits and liabilities, when
there are assets like hers around!

He is off, leaving George to gape at his wake.

12. FULL SHOT ANN

She is seated now, fussing over the desk as she prepares to get to work. Abruptly, Roger appears behind her, tenderly covers her two eyes with one hand, while the other reaches around to lay the present before her.

      ROGER
Guess who.

      ANN
    (coyly)
...Roger?

      ROGER
    (removes his hand)
Happy Birthday to the prettiest girl in this
entire office!

      ANN
    (flirting)
I am the *only* girl.

                              ROGER
                       (flamboyantly gallant)
                And you'd remain the prettiest, if this office were
                staffed with the assembled Miss Americas of the
                past five years! Now stop begging compliments
                and open your present!

The girl grins, eagerly pulls away the wrapping, and "Ooooohs" with delight.

                               ANN
                     Roger! It's beautiful!

13.   FULL SHOT GEORGE

As he rises from extracting his own gift from the desk drawer. There is a look of expectation on his face as he lays it on the desk, looks up to see what Roger has given.

14.   ANGLE ON ANN

She holds a sheer silk peignoir against herself, preening.

15.   FULL SHOT GEORGE

He reacts, his face paling up at the brazen gift and its reception; he leans heavily against his desk. The gift-wrapped package containing his gift rests beside him and he pauses, the box juggles on the desk, unnoticed by George. It is as if the contents were human, and restless.

16.   CLOSE SHOT BOX

It bobbles again, and from the bottom a small, puff of smoke escapes, like a fluff of cotton candy rising on a breeze. It dissipates almost as quickly as it appears.

17.   BACK TO ANN

She nods regally to the office staff, assembled to admire and congratulate her. Sam is the office buffoon.

                               SAM
                Hey, Ann, put it on! Can you feature Old Man

Watson's puss when he calls you in for dictation?

Appreciative guffaws greet this sally.

                      ANN
               (parrying expertly)
Mr. Watson is interested in a different kind of figure, Sam!

                    ROGER
               (hinting)
You like it, Ann?

                    ANN
I love it! But you shouldn't have been so extravagant!

                    ROGER
You only have a birthday once a year...
               (winks)
until you're thirty. Then you have them once every two years!

                    ANN
Come here, Roger!

She suddenly reaches out, embraces him and kisses him full on the lips; no little peck, no embarrassment at the audience. There are whistles from the jealous bachelors and the wistful husbands.

18.   CLOSE SHOT – GEORGE

He reacts, chagrined, then reaches for his own gift, determined not to be outdone.

19.   ANGLE – FAVORING ANN

As she wipes the lipstick from Roger's grinning mouth. George edges his way to the periphery of the group.

                    ANN
That's to show my appreciation...and to prove I haven't even learned how to *count* to thirty yet!

Abruptly, there is a monumental clearing of a throat, and every head turns toward it as if attached by a single wire; a Pavlovian response.

20. FULL SHOT MR. WATSON

He moves to Ann's desk, fixing them with baleful eye.

> ANN
> (shakily)
> Mr. Watson!...it's my birthday...

Mr. Watson wears a vest and conservative suit. He seems past the age, or at least the inclination of frivolity, much less lechery. At the moment he also wears a deep, dark frown of approval.

> WATSON
> Do any of you happen to be aware of the annual statement issued by this organization... on Miss Lawson's birthday?

He glances at them, giving each the impression that he has somehow been derelict in his duty, if not downright subversive, as far as the organization is concerned.

21. PAN SHOT

> The group hangs its collective head.

22. BACK TO WATSON

> WATSON
> No one?
> (a beat, then his eyes begin
> to twinkle)
> Then I'm sure it will come as an agreeable surprise that this company just completed the best year in its history. I believe this department had no small part in that success.

There are murmurs of pleasant surprise.

                    WATSON (CONT'D)
            So, as a token of my personal appreciation...
                    (he breaks down and grins happily)
            I think this is an appropriate time to invite all
            of you to be my guests for a celebration party,
            beginning as fast as we can meet at the Tiki Club!

23.   ANGLE ON THE GROUP

Ad lib reactions: "I'm for it," "I never thought he had it in him," etc. But Watson holds up his hand for silence. Ann hugs him impulsively and kisses his cheek.

                    ANN
            You're a doll, Mr. Watson!

                    WATSON
                    (beaming)
            And as for you, young lady.... They aren't the
            only ones who appreciate you!

With this, he pulls open the door to his office and reaches inside, reappearing the next instant with a truly beautiful, goblet-shaped, crystal vase, brimful of perfect red roses. Ann is astonished.

                    WATSON
            Happy birthday, to the best-looking *and* the
            hardest working secretary I ever had!

                    ANN
            Oh! They're gorgeous!

24.   CLOSE SHOT GEORGE

As he sinks, slowly below the horizon, outmaneuvered, out-bought, out, period.

25.   ANGLE ON GROUP

As they begin to disburse, heading for the hall door, Ann hesitates a moment, setting the vase on her desk and admiring it, then she starts to follow, with Roger hovering near.

                    ROGER
        Let's go, kid, before the old man discovers he's
        off his nut and has himself committed!

                    ANN
                 (defensive)
        He's a sweet, dear man!

26.   ANGLE ON GEORGE

Standing morose and almost alone, as Ann and Roger start out. As they move past, he finds his voice.

                    GEORGE
        Happy…happy birthday, Ann.

                    ANN
                  (warmly)
        George, thank you! Aren't you coming?

                    GEORGE
        I'll be along…

                    ANN
                (breezing on)
        See you there! Come on, Roger.

Roger gives him a broad wink, mouths "more equal," and points to himself as he exits with her.

27.   HIGH ANGLE THE OFFICE

As George forlornly retreats to his desk, sadly retrieves his present, and moves with it to her desk, repeating his action at the top of the act when he anticipated the gift-giving so eagerly. Now he holds the gift and stares at what Roger and Mr. Watson bestowed on his goddess.

28.   FULL SHOT

Wistfully he reflects on his usual state: dead last, no matter how small the field. Compared to Roger's gift, his is downright avuncular; compared to Mr. Watson's, it is puny and insulting. For a moment he starts to toss it into the trash pail, then shrugs.

>   GEORGE
>   (rueful reflection)
>   Maybe I can use it for an ashtray or something…

He starts out of the office now, glances back, and dutifully clicks out all the lights, before closing the door behind him. CAMERA HOLDS THE HANDSOME and daring gifts on Ann's desk, before we

>   DISSOLVE TO:

29.   INT GEORGE'S APT NIGHT

It is dominated by his bachelorhood and his hobbies. Things lie where they fall in George's living room, not messy, but comfortably cluttered. Books are piled on most available flat surfaces, including the floor; Attila, a mongrel mutt, betrays his ferocious name by bounding from his accustomed place in the center of a small couch, to greet his master with docile affection; along one wall, a large framed glass case holds George's extensive butterfly collection. George drops the package on the couch after patting Attila, then moves to hang his coat in the closet and toss his tie over a chair. Through this he carries on a necessarily one-sided conversation with Attila, who has promptly returned to the couch, near the package.

>   GEORGE
>   Hello boy. Have a good day? Mine was lousy!
>   I couldn't even enjoy a party, watching that Roger.
>   (he turns to the closet)
>   Why does it always happen to me, Attila? Some
>   people, they're born with a silver spoon in their
>   mouths; I must have been born with egg on my
>   face… Now I didn't give her *any* present!

30.   FULL SHOT ATTILA

He lolls on the couch, listening with an understanding ear. Beside him, the package begins to bobble and wriggle as it did in the office, and attracts his nose to the alien presence. Attila circles around the package with that peculiarly canine mixture of suspicion and curiosity. He seems to be trying to make up his mind if it is to be eaten, chased, or used for ablutions.

                    GEORGE (VO)
         I know what they all think I am: a patsy, a jerk!
         Especially Roger.
                    (a beat)
         And they're right. What a purpose in life.

31.   CLOSE SHOT GEORGE

Coming back into the room from the closet.

                    GEORGE
         George P. Hanley, vocation, jerk!

His speculation is interrupted by a growl from Attila. He looks up sharply.

32.   CLOSE SHOT ATTILA

Backing away from the package. He growls again…but continues backing away.

33.   ANGLE ON GEORGE

As he moves forward.

                    GEORGE
                    (ruefully)
         Attila! You'll give yourself a trauma! You can't
         growl and back away at the same time! Be brave!

He approaches, reassuring, but Attila slinks off, coward that he knows himself to be.

                    GEORGE (CONT'D)
                    (fondly)
         We're two of a kind. Come on, I'll show you.

He slumps on the couch and pulls the lamp out of the box.

                    GEORGE (CONT'D)
         See? It's only a box with this beat-up old lamp in
         it. Probably came from some junkyard!

Attila decides it's safe enough to come out from behind the stuffed chair he has used to hide behind. He appears, sheepishly.

> GEORGE (CONT'D)
> (holds it out)
> See? "A magnificent old antique," "rare distinction"...
> (at himself)
> Boy, if being a jerk is my vocation, at least I'm good at it! Look, it's so tarnished, it's almost black.

Attila, encouraged now, comes up, sniffs it, and wags his tail. He barks.

> GEORGE
> That's telling them! But a little late, Attila! Like me! Let's clean it up, anyway.

He looks for something to polish it, finds a soiled shirt on a chair, shrugs, and gives the lamp a few brisk rubs with it.

> GEORGE (CONT'D)
> I guess it's old, all right. If dirt's any sign!

He rubs again, this time with both hands.

34.   ANGLE FEATURING LAMP AND GEORGE

There is a sudden rumbling SOUND, and something causes George to drop the lamp onto the couch beside him. The noise is a very modern percussive concatenation, such as is dear to hi-fi buffs, like four men playing glass tumblers and a set of bongos. From the lamp, a trickle of smoke rises, as from a burning cigarette, then shapes into a distinct, small mushroom shape.

35.   ANGLE ON GEORGE

Reacting, mouth open, too astonished to be frightened.

36.   ANGLE ON SMOKE CLOUD

From the cloud materializes a very modern, very effete genie, sitting on the couch. He is of indeterminate years, with crew-cut hair, wears a Brooks' Bros. blazer displaying an emblem on the pocket, button-down shirt and thin tie.

                    GENIE
            (bored)
        You would have to do that.

37.   TWO SHOT GEORGE & GENIE

                    GEORGE
        Who…who…who…
            (gulps)

The Genie crosses his knees, smothers a yawn.

                    GENIE
        I'm the Genie of the lamp, of course. Aladdin.
        Magic…that whole bit.

                    GEORGE
        Aladdin's lamp? It's real? It really exists?

                    GENIE
        Thank heaven I don't have to go through all that.
        You're reasonably perceptive. That box kept
        brushing against the lamp. Gave me indigestion.

                    GEORGE
        But…you don't *look* like a Genie!

                    GENIE
            (shrugs)
        I am. In the old days, people wanted whatever
        the Sultan had, so we appeared in the image of
        the Sultan's for credibility. Times change; we try
        to keep up.

                    GEORGE
            (getting excited)
        If you're the genie…then I'm…the master of the lamp!

                    GENIE
            (delicately wipes his forehead
            with breast pocket paisley)
        We'd prefer you don't use that word, "master".

Passé, you know. Smacks of being anti-liberal.
Why don't you think of yourself as an…
administrative supervisor?

GEORGE

But what about my wishes? There's supposed to
be three wishes.

GENIE

Only in the days of conspicuous consumption;
you get one wish, Mr. Hanley.

GEORGE

One?

GENIE

Inflation. And the threat of automation, of course.

GEORGE

Oh, of course…

GENIE

We hope to get a better class of wishes that way.

GEORGE

I see…

GENIE

Give it some thought. Toss all your ideas into
the hopper; mull them over. Then run a wish or
two up the flagpole, and see which one you feel
like saluting. When you've decided, summon me.
        (sighs)
And please be good enough to wait until you're *sure*.
This childish smoke-screen routine embarrasses me.

GEORGE

Couldn't you be…sort of available? For consultation?

GENIE

No offense, but to be perfectly frank, it's a bore,
this endlessly ministering to the whims of mankind.

When you've seen one millennium, you've seen them all.

                    GEORGE

But ever since I was a boy, I read a lot, and I used to dream what I wanted to do when I grew up…

                    GENIE

Hardly unique!

                    GEORGE

Yes, but it's *my* wish. And all my life, I've wanted *three* things.

                    GENIE

I know, I know. Throughout my career, there have been *no* original wishes. The same three, over and over. Oh, the frills might change, the description differs…but the paucity of imagination!

                    GEORGE

You…can't help me decide?

                    GENIE

Sorry. Helping went out with turbans and loin cloths. I'm off. Please do try not call me till you're certain.
        (a small grimace)
The change from ectoplasm to substance is rather bad for my liver.

As George stares, he disappears to the accompaniment of the percussion and the mushroom cloud, which funnels itself back into the lamp.

38.   ANGLE ON GEORGE

                    GEORGE

Aladdin's lamp!…Me, with Aladdin's lamp!

He scurries to the lamp, which Attila is now sniffing at, plucks it away from him, holding it with the care he'd lavish on crystal.

GEORGE (CONT'D)
You better keep away from it, Attila. You might
lick it into making the Genie appear before I'm ready.

He finds a secure place for it on a bookshelf, stands staring at it.

GEORGE (CONT'D)
I can't believe it! Anything I want in the whole
world! Anything!

He relishes the thought a moment, then his elation begins to change to a frown. He kneels beside the dog, and begins to stroke its head.

GEORGE (CONT'D)
But only *one* wish. Which one, Attila? Which one?

FADE OUT:

FADE IN: ACT II

39.   INT. GEORGE'S APARTMENT ANGLE ON ATTILA NIGHT

He lies curled in his favorite spot on the couch, head nestled between his forepaws, snoozing. CAMERA SLOWLY TRUCKS ACROSS the dimly lighted room, to stop at CLOSE SHOT OF GEORGE. He sits in the big chair, his head thrown back, eyes closed, mouth open. Clutched tightly in his hands is the magic lamp, held against his middle protectively. George wears a beautiful smile of contentment, for he is dreaming. SLOWLY CAMERA PUSHES INTO GEORGE'S FACE. The image shimmers, then the entire picture dissolves into George's dream.

DISSOLVE TO:

40.   EXT. MOVIE SOUNDSTAGE ANGLE AT ENTRANCE DOOR

A large sign proclaims a closed set; the flashing red light is for the moment still as George Hanley walks briskly and confidently to the door, and ignoring the sign, enters the studio.

41.   INT. SOUNDSTAGE

George enters, moves confidently toward the center of activity. (NOTE: WHATEVER LAVISH LOOKING SET IS AVAILABLE SHOULD BE SEEN IN THIS SCENE AS THE BACKGROUND SET OF WHICH EVERYONE IS WORKING.) He pauses a moment beaming his admiration, and basking in pride of ownership.

42.   ANGLE ON BACKGROUND SET

Peering into a hand mirror held by a hairdresser (THE GIFT SHOP PROPRIETOR) is Ann Alexandra, a young woman who by no coincidence in this dream, bears a striking resemblance to Ann Lawson, but more sophisticated, and if possible, more dazzling. She pats and puffs a few infinitesimal imperfections into place. Her costume should be appropriate to the background set; something sexy for a love scene. The director chats with her.

                       DIRECTOR
        Remember, Miss Alexandra: you love this guy
        so much, your guts do a loop the loop as soon
        as you smell his after shave lotion!

She turns to him, arching her neck and shoulders to relieve tired muscles. On her the movement looks very appealing.

                         ANN
        I'll try...
            (seeing George O.C.)
        Darling!

George enters frame, smiles, shyly. The director barely notices him with a nod as he moves off.

                       GEORGE
        Hello, dear.

She takes both his hands in hers as he bends close to kiss her.

                       ANN
            (warning)
        Makeup, Georgie.

43.   CLOSE TWO SHOT GEORGE & ANN

George stops, lips puckered, an inch from her face.

ANN
(teasing)
You wouldn't want me to play my final scene with smeared lipstick?

GEORGE
(glumly)
No. I guess not..."*Final*" scene?

ANN
(takes his arm, cooing)
It's been a long grind!

GEORGE
It sure has! They said you could take a few weeks off: that was six *months* ago.

ANN
(innocently)
Well, we could take our honeymoon now...if you want to, of course...

GEORGE
Want to!
(reaches out to embrace her)

ANN
Georgie!

He stops just in time.

GEORGE
(petulant)
Makeup all day; beauty creams all night!

ANN
A movie star isn't paid to look ugly, baby! Besides...
(coyly)
...don't you think I'm worth waiting for?

                        GEORGE
            Yeah, sure.
                (plaintively)
            But six months…!

                        DIRECTOR (OC)
            Places. Let's go!

44.   FULL SHOT ANN

                        ANN
                (lets her hand linger in his)
            I won't be long.

She breaks away, turns to toss him a small, personal kiss with her fingertips.

CAMERA PUSHES INTO GEORGE

He smiles a Cheshire cat smile

                                        DISSOLVE TO:

45.   OMIT

46.   INT STAR DRESSING ROOM ANGLE ON MIRROR

This is a large room, dominated by a mirror and an enormous bed. It is a feminine room in décor and in feeling, with one gesture in George's direction, his favorite armchair from the apartment. But even this is not inviolate since it has female clothing tossed over it casually. A zoo of stuffed animals graces the pillows. CAMERA PANS THE ROOM TO TAKE IT IN, ENDS ON THE DOORWAY THROUGH WHICH ENTER ANN AND GEORGE.

47.   ANGLE ON ANN & GEORGE

He carries her fur coat, plus two large overnight cases and a hatbox. She wears a skin tight lounge suit.

                        ANN
            What a day. What a trying, endless day!

George closes the door, turns to see her moving across the room. The sight makes him swallow hard.

48.   ANGLE ON ANN'S BACK   HIS POV

As she undulates across the room, the high heels and tight suit lending seductive grace to her swaying rump.

49.   ANGLE ON GEORGE

He dumps the things on a chair, follows her.

>   GEORGE
> Tonight, no crawling into bed right after dinner to study your lines; tomorrow morning…no getting up at four-thirty to get to the studio for makeup!

He reaches to embrace her.

>   GEORGE (CONT'D)
> I like your face, just the way it is…

She yawns almost in his face.

>   ANN
> Sorry, darling…

She crosses away from him to a dressing-room alcove. CAMERA HOLDS GEORGE WHO SLUMPS TO THE BED, DEFEATED

>   ANN (O.C.)
> I'm just worn out from that ersatz D. W. Griffith howling all day.

>   GEORGE
> I thought you liked him.

>   ANN (O.C.)
> I suppose. But he's so *noisy*: he thinks you measure virility in decibels. He'll be a lot quieter at the party.

                          GEORGE
            What party?

                          ANN (O.C)
            Did you forget? The celebration party on the set
            tonight.

                          GEORGE
            Oh yeah…

Smiles and rises to cross to her.

50.   ANGLE IN ALCOVE

Ann has removed the lounge suit, and donned a figure defying Muumuu. As George moves to her, she sits before a dressing table with a large mirror, and briskly covers her hair with a voluminous net.

                          GEORGE
            We'll leave the party early.

He bends over her shoulder, arms around her to embrace, leans over her to kiss her mouth. But as he approached, she has dipped her hand in a jar of cold cream, scooped up a blob of it, and suddenly raised it to remove her lipstick. Their two actions synchronize so that George's lips, expecting to savor hers, savor cold cream instead.

                          ANN
            George!

51.   CLOSE SHOT GEORGE

He winces at the greasy taste, wipes it away.

52.   TWO SHOT

Without a pause, Ann has continued, now rubs vigorously at her mouth to remove the lipstick. With her other hand, she gestures to the center of her forehead, half turns her face up, but continues her task.

                          ANN
            Careful of my hair, baby. There'll be a million

photographers tonight: Andre would have a
convulsion if it's ruined!

George bends down and plants the antiseptic kiss as indicated, then backs off defeated.

> GEORGE
> (bitterly)
> Andre should carry medical insurance!

All this has happened quickly, Ann performing her tasks without missing a beat.

> ANN
> (sitting up)
> What I want right now is a nice hot bath for
> about an hour.

She starts for the door to the bathroom, unbuttoning.

> GEORGE
> (left at the post)
> You want me to...rub your back?

> ANN
> No, why don't you...
> (a tiny beat)
> take the dog for a walk. He's been cooped up
> all day.

She closes the door behind her.

53.   FULL SHOT   GEORGE

He stands there a moment, then resigned, moves across the room, whistling.

> GEORGE
> Here, boy...come on, boy.

He picks up a leather leash with a jeweled collar clasp.

> GEORGE
> Outside. Come on,...snap it up!

He bends down to snap the leash, obscuring the animal.

>   GEORGE (CONT'D)
>   Let's go,...
>   (ruefully)
>   Attila!

As he rises, we see George is bent over a vast dog-bed basket, and reclining on a velvet pillow indolently, is an elegant, carefully cut and groomed French poodle. He leads the animal out the door.

>   DISSOLVE TO:

54.   INT SOUNDSTAGE ANGLE ON SET

A large, bubbling party in full gavotte, overflows the set seen earlier. Little knots of well-groomed people laugh at each others inanities; while strolling alone, with hands in pockets on the periphery of these groups, is George. Just George, very much alone, and feeling lost.

55.   FULL SHOT GEORGE

He hesitates at one small group, but someone's back quickly fills a momentary opening. George moves on and is hailed by Eli Watson (Mr. Watson from the office), dressed in black suit, white-on-white shirt and white tie. He is shrewd.

>   WATSON
>   George, boy!
>   (leading him to a corner)

I've gotta talk to you. Ann mentioned something about you needing a vacation...

>   GEORGE
>   (grinning)
>   Not me; her. Both of us. Together!

56.   TWO SHOT IN A CORNER OF THE SET

>   WATSON
>   I'm not gonna mince words. You gotta say it's
>   okay for Ann to do my next picture, "Beowulf."

GEORGE
Not a chance...
   (shyly)
It's our honeymoon!

WATSON
Great! I'm shooting "Beowulf" on location: make a great honeymoon!

GEORGE
Some honeymoon...Makeup call at four-thirty AM? Work all day? Study lines all night? For the last six months the only times I saw her when she wasn't sleeping, she was getting herself swabbed with makeup or beauty creams or rinses or some other stuff!

WATSON
She's a star. You wouldn't want her photographed with bags under her eyes and wrinkles! How would you like to see her like that? Eh?

GEORGE
I just want to see her *alone*...even with bags and wrinkles!

WATSON
My boy, the world is full of "have-nots". *You* are a "Have"! You want the world's most beautiful woman for a wife, you've got to share her with the world!

GEORGE
I did! For six months! Now I want the world to share her back!

WATSON
   (sadly)
Son, it's not for myself. But no Ann, no Beowulf!" Know how many good people will be trudging up and down unemployment lines? Actors—grips—prop men?—
   (tenderly)

They've got wives and sweethearts! They've got little ones! They've got mortgages, and sports cars to pay for!

              GEORGE
           (weakening)
There are other stars.

              WATSON
Not like Ann Alexandra. Millions of plain folks all over the world wait to see her. Little kids count their pennies; mothers go without lunch; brave men sacrifice even the tiny luxury of a cigarette so they can buy a ticket to a movie theatre and escape the drab drudgery of an uncaring world by watching their idol, Ann Alexandra, looking like a fairytale, doing all the things they dream, but never get to do…

              GEORGE
           (seeing it)
I know…

              WATSON
           (passionately; a tear in his voice)
For them, George…the salt of the earth! Couldn't you find it in your heart to make this…*one, little* sacrifice?

              GEORGE
           (moved)
You're right, Mr. Watson. I'll tell her she can make the picture. We'll make the sacrifice…together!

He turns, moves off into the throng. Watson watches, then reacts, preening himself.

              WATSON
I should cast *myself* in this picture! Wonder how I'd look with a sword?

57.   ANGLE ON WAITER

He holds a tray with several glasses of champagne. George strides into frame, notice his wife O.C., plucks two glasses from the tray.

58.   ANGLE ON ANN & ROGER

She is gloriously gowned; Roger Andrews, the male star, with graying temples, faultless tailoring, is a suave, Hollywood version of Roger Hackett. He turns, just as George approaches, eyes glued to the full glasses he is attempting to balance while walking.

>   ROGER
> Ladies and Gentlemen...I'd like to make an
> announcement.

59.   ANGLE OVER BACKS OF CROWD

To see Roger and Ann, her hand on his arm, George halts with glasses frozen in mid-air. There is a delighted gasp, then expectant silence.

>   ROGER
> I'll make a toast.

He turns toward George, and with hardly a pause, lifts the two glasses right out of his hands, swings back to Ann and continues.

>   ROGER
> ...thanks old man...
>   (hands one to her, raises his)

To the brightest star, the most exciting leading lady, the loveliest woman, in the world. Ann Alexandra...who has just agreed to star with me in Beowulf."

60.   ANGLE ON GEORGE

As people around him all raise their glasses, and drink, he looks at his hands, lets them flutter to his side helplessly.

61.   ANGLE ON ROGER & ANN

He looks at her as the crowd applauds heartily. A photographer motions them together, then sights through his camera. She beams up at Roger, moves into his arms as if they were a matched set. He turns his face to kiss her, but, she shakes her head no.

>   ANN (sotto voice)
>   Makeup, darling. Besides I'm not as good in
>   profile.

Then she lays her cheek beside his to provide two beaming faces, head on, for the photographers.

62.   ANGLE ON GEORGE

He frowns, then glumly turns and walks away. He moves to a vacant corner of the set, finds a grand piano, sinks wearily to the bench. Then seeing a full drink set on the top of the piano, he looks for its owner. Not finding one, he reaches for the drink, sips it.

>   STARLET (O.C.)
>   Stop, thief!

>   GEORGE
>   (looks around startled)
>   Who's that?

63.   ANGLE TO SEE STARLET

As she climbs out from underneath the piano. She is the young, bovine type, with a magnificent figure, an aggressive manner and the mind of a cash register. She also has a hot-house Italian accent.

>   STARLET
>   Me, Mister.

>   GEORGE
>   Were you hiding?

>   STARLET
>   I snap something. Nobody down on that level…
>   yet.

>   GEORGE
>   Make your…repairs?

STARLET
I have always accidents; how you say – I am too much…prone?

GEORGE
(blushing slightly)
I see…want your drink back?

STARLET
(petulant)
It's only to hold. I'm under the age.

GEORGE
(dumb)
Under the age?

STARLET
(archly)
To drink. I have a problem…In years, I'm still a child; but I think I'm mature. Don't you think I'm…mature?

GEORGE
I…guess so.

STARLET
You are a producer…no?

GEORGE
Me?
(shakes his head)
Nope.

STARLET
Director?

GEORGE
No.

STARLET
(a beat)
A writer?

                    GEORGE
        Sorry.

                    STARLET
        Then I cannot guess — who you are?

                    GEORGE
        George Hanley.

                    STARLET
        Who?

                    GEORGE
        I'm Ann Alexandra's husband.

                    STARLET
              (dropping all pretense)
        Oh, for Pete's sake. Gimme my drink back!

She grabs for it, and George in his shyness and embarrassment stumbles, getting the drink down the front of his clothes.

        Serves ya right! For wasting my time! *Mister* Alexandra!

She stalks off, leaving a rueful George.

64.   FULL SHOT GEORGE

He stares after her a moment. Then he stands up on the bench, looking over the crowd.

                    GEORGE
              (calls)
        Ann? Ann...
              (to himself)
        Where'd she get to now?

Unable to spot her, he notes a high stepladder standing close to the flats forming the rear wall of the set. He goes to it.

65.   ANGLE ON LADDER

As George climbs up a few rungs to get a better vantage point. He shades his eyes with his hand, suddenly stiffens as he hears voices from behind the flats: soft, intimate voices.

> ROGER (O.C.)
> Now aren't you glad you came tonight?

> ANN (O.C.)
> Don't be egotistical. I had to come anyway.

George hesitates, then quietly ascends another rung or two until he can see over the top of the flats. Over this the conversation continues.

> ROGER
> I don't understand you.

> ANN
> No man is supposed to. That's the way we little girls are.

> ROGER
> That part I understand.

66.   ANGLE ON ROGER AND ANN

In the shadows behind the set, in ardent embrace.

> ANN
> You mean George?

> ROGER
> Yes!

67.   CLOSE SHOT GEORGE

He is pale, but straining to hear, like a prisoner already pronounced guilty, but waiting for the judges and sentence.

> ANN (V.O.)
> He's the *perfect* husband!

                    ROGER (V.O.)
             That absurd little mouse?

68.   ANGLE ON ANN & ROGER

                         ANN
                      (smiles)
             A handy excuse when I need one. And when I
             don't...no impediment.

She pulls his head down to kiss him, but Roger puts her off.

                        ROGER
                      (teasing)
             I'll spoil your makeup...

                         ANN
             Who cares!

And she kisses him, with shocking disregard for the "have-not" millions and especially the have-not husband.

69.   FULL SHOT GEORGE

He raises his hands, clenches and unclenches them in painful frustration; tears of hurt forming in his eyes. Then blindly starting to move down, he stumbles

                                        QUICK CUT TO:

70.   REVERSE ANGLE

To see George losing his balance, teetering against the ladder the bright lights beginning to whirl behind him.

                                        QUICK CUT TO:

71.   FULL SHOT GEORGE

             He topples over.

                                        QUICK CUT TO:

72.	CLOSE SHOT GEORGE'S FACE (INT. GEORGE'S ROOM)

As it falls into frame, upside down. The effect of the cuts should be that he is falling through space. But his head comes to rest full frame, upside down. His eyes pop open and stare. After a beat, the face of the real Attila pushes into frame and licks his master.

73.	ANGLE ON GEORGE

He has fallen straight backwards in the deep chair he has been dreaming in, and fallen to the floor unhurt. He lies there an instant, recovering his bearings, and then sighs in relief. Then he pulls himself into a comfortable position sitting on the floor, pats Attila's head reassuringly.

> GEORGE
> Whew! A dream.

74.	ANOTHER ANGLE

He rises, finds the lamp on the floor where it has fallen, inspects it.

> GEORGE
> (turns to the dog)
> Know something, Attila? That's the trouble for a...a guy like me. Having something I want so much...only means it'd hurt that much more to lose it!

He slumps down on the couch, staring at the lamp, dejected.

> GEORGE (CONT'D)
> And I *would* lose a wife like that.... Might as well face it.

The dog comes to him, shoves its snoot under his hand, asking to be petted.

> GEORGE (CONT'D)
> *You* still love me, huh? Thanks!
> (beat)
> Well...at least it should make the choice easier. Now I've only got to decide between the other two things I always wanted!

FADE OUT.

ACT III

FADE IN:

75. INT ACCOUNTING OFFICE MORNING

George strides to his desk, head up, almost cocky; passing Miss Lawson, who is getting ready for the morning's work at her desk, he pauses, about to bid her a cheerful good morning, then reminded of her falseness, abruptly turns away from her and to his desk.

>   GEORGE
>   (cheerily)
>   Good morning, Roger!
>
>   ROGER
>   'Morning.
>   (edgily)
>   Well, today's the day.
>
>   GEORGE
>   (rubs hands, sits)
>   For what, Rog?
>
>   ROGER
>   (a beat, eyes him narrowly)
>   What's got into *you*?
>
>   GEORGE
>   Me? All I said was "good morning," and "for what?" Rog. I didn't think they were such pregnant phrases.
>
>   ROGER
>   (comes to him, peers narrowly)
>   You're real feisty this morning, George old Porgie! Has Watson spoke to you about that promotion?
>
>   GEORGE
>   (realizing)

Oh, the promotion. I was forgetting...

ROGER

I'll bet!

ANN
(calling O.C.)
Roger! ...Mr. Watson would like you in his office

ROGER
(reacts, anticipating)
Right away!
(to George)
This could be *it*! Well...over the top!

GEORGE
(to himself)
They'd *never* pick him! Never!

He shrugs, settles down at the desk, pulls out some papers, but is interrupted by the appearance of Sam at his elbow thrusting a ledger and a folder at him.

SAM

George, the old boy wants another check on all these entries.

GEORGE

What for?

SAM

New account; Personal. This guy is so loaded he could pay off the national debt out of petty cash!

GEORGE

Didn't you double-check after you made the entries?

SAM

Sure.

GEORGE

Then why again, Sam. It's not efficient; it's a waste of time!

                        SAM
            How much do you make a week?

                       GEORGE
            Same as you. Ninety-eight fifty.

                        SAM
            My boy, this joker makes so much dough, he
            sweats more than ninety-eight bucks every time he
            ties his shoelaces! So waste a little time!

He dumps the things on George's desk, and bounces off. George shrugs, reaches for the ledger and idly opens to the last page. He stares at the figures, does a take.

76.   INSERT SHOT CU LEDGER PAGE

What stands out is the bottom line that indicates:
            Net Worth: $26,832,461.

77.   CU GEORGE

He whistles softly between his teeth. Then he reflects, staring off into space. The image shimmers, then DISSOLVE THROUGH TO THE DAYDREAM.

78.   EXT CITY STREET HIGH ANGLE

A gleaming Rolls-Royce slips to the curb, and halts. Its uniformed chauffeur jumps out, hustles around to open the passenger door.

79.   EXT STREET ANGLE ON CAR

With a respectful bow, the liveried driver holds the door, as an expensively tailored man of means, wearing gloves and sporting a walking cane, pops out. It is G. Peter Hanley, a touch plumper now from good living. He surveys the day a moment. NOTE: G. PETER SHOULD BE PLAYED WITH WALTER MITTYESQUE SANS FREUD.

                      CHAUFFEUR
            Nice day, isn't it?

                    GEORGE
    It'll do.

                    CHAUFFEUR
    Will you be wanting me for lunch, sir?

                    GEORGE
    Oh…I can't say. You'd better be available, just
    in case, Roger.

80.   ANGLE TO SEE CHAUFFEUR

As he salutes. It is indeed Roger Hackett, servant now to wealthy George.

                    CHAUFFEUR
    Of course, sir.

He starts to slam the door behind George, but an enormous dog pops out of the car, dashing after George.

81.   ANGLE ON GEORGE, DOG AND CHAUFFEUR

The animal is an enormous Afghan hound, that rare breed with the long snoot, heavy coat and almost absurdly slender body. Roger steps up apologetically.

                    GEORGE
                (fondling dog)
    Oh no, boy. I can't play now.

                    CHAUFFEUR
    I'm sorry. I couldn't hold him Mr. Hanley.

                    GEORGE
    Take Attila over to 21 and have the chef pick him
    out a nice prime rib. Not too fatty.

                    CHAUFFEUR
    Yes sir.

He takes the animal by the collar as George turns for an afterthought.

> GEORGE
> And you better trot him around the block a few
> times. His appetite's a little jaded.

He moves off, leaving the chauffeur to sigh, wearily.

82. EXT BUSINESS BUILDING

As George steps up briskly. A prominent plaque identifies the structure as the HANLEY BUILDING. George squints at it in satisfaction as he pauses before entering the revolving door. Just then a small newsboy staggers up, barely equal to the load of papers he bears. He is ragged, thin, the vision of Horatio Alger.

> NEWSBOY
> (puffing)
> Paper, sir?...Paper?

George turns and looks down at the tyke, ruffling his hair paternally.

> GEORGE
> How old are you, son?

> NEWSBOY
> Nine, sir.

> GEORGE
> Nine!
> (fondly)
> I see you here every morning...don't you miss school?

> NEWSBOY
> Oh no, sir. I wouldn't miss school! I get up at five for my papers, then I go to the afternoon session at PS 31.

> GEORGE
> Incredible! What do your parents say?

> NEWSBOY
> (bravely)
> My mama's dead...my old man had a store, but

it went broke.

>GEORGE
>I'm sorry…I'll have a paper.

>NEWSBOY
>Yes, sir.

The boy cheerfully reaches a paper, and takes the bill offered, then fumbles to reach a change-maker at his belt. Suddenly he drops his papers, staring at the bill in astonishment.

>NEWSBOY (CONT'D)
>(awed)
>Gosh, I can't change a hundred dollar bill.

>GEORGE
>(benignly)
>I didn't expect you to, son!

And he turns, enters the building leaving the gaping recipient of his largesse.

83. INT HALLWAY ANGLE ON PANELLED DOOR

Gold letters identify this as the door to: GEORGE P. HANELY, PRIVATE SUITE. A gloved hand turns the handle and George P. himself, enters.

84. INT SUITE

As he enters. This is the ultra modern kind of living room-office. Elegant furniture; heavy carpeting and drapes, no desk except a massive refectory table at one end where Mr. Hanley reigns when in residence. Pulling the drapes to reveal the view of the city, is Miss Lawson, tailored suit, severe hair style, glasses, etc., the perfect dedicated, no-nonsense, executive secretary.

>MISS LAWSON
>Good morning, sir. Tri Electronics up seven-eights on the morning ticker. Glad to see you back.

>GEORGE
>Thank you.

MISS LAWSON
How was the Riviera?

GEORGE
(removing his gloves, pulling at
each fingertip)
All right, I guess. It's kind of like a suburban tract, only all castles.

MISS LAWSON
Gay, social whirl, wasn't it, sir?

GEORGE
I was about whirled out after the first six parties. They even had one to celebrate the tide coming in on time!
(notes a spot on his glove)
Miss Lawson, would you take care of these? They're soiled.

He reaches the gloves to Miss Lawson, who nods dutifully, takes the gloves by the thumbs, like a dead fish, and daintily drops them in a wastebasket, with a thud.

MISS LAWSON
(through above action)
Certainly, Mr. Hanley.

GEORGE
(startled)
Can't they be cleaned?

MISS LAWSON
We throw them away, sir: in your tax bracket, it's cheaper.

GEORGE
Oh…

He sits at the table giving cursory attention to some papers.

MISS LAWSON
Shall I start the people in?

GEORGE
Might as well.

She moves off to a door leading to an outer office, and is almost immediately replaced by an elderly man who moves to George with a deferential sir, a distinguished looking Mr. Watson.

GEORGE
(surprised)
Doctor Watson! What are you doing here?

WATSON
Begging again, I'm afraid. These days a college president is much more concerned with salesmanship than scholarship.

GEORGE
You came to the right man.

WATSON
(delicately)
Mr. Hanley, you've already done more for your alma mater than we have a right to ask; this is an emergency or I wouldn't be here.

GEORGE
(grins)
How much?

WATSON
Too much! But I'm hoping you'll be able to start the ball rolling.

GEORGE
Don't be coy, sir. How much?
Takes out checkbook, begins to fill in a check.

WATSON
Altogether, one million two hundred thousand. Now, if you could possibly start us off with say, ten or twenty thousand...

                    GEORGE
          You've got it.
               (finishes scribbling)

                    WATSON
          You're a generous man, G.P. We're all in your debt.
               (glances at the check, reacts)
          But you've made a mistake, man!

George puts his arm around the gentleman's shoulder, walks with him to the door.

                    GEORGE
          No, I've always been good with figures.

                    WATSON
          It's the entire sum! One million, two hundred thousand!

                    GEORGE
               (a beat; then modestly)
          It's deductible.

Watson draws himself up with dramatic intensity.

                    WATSON
          No, sir. I can't take this.

                    GEORGE
          But, I *want* to give it.

                    WATSON
               (gently lectures)
          So would others, Mr. Hanley! Thousands of alumni, not as successful, not as…fortunate, but every bit as generous. Giving…sharing the burden *and* the satisfaction…is the cement which binds their minds and hearts to our beloved alma mater!
               (returns check)
          I can't let you deprive them of the great privilege of giving!

GEORGE
I just wanted to help.

WATSON
This isn't generosity, G.P.; it's ostentation!

GEORGE
(humbly)
I'm sorry... What should I do?

WATSON
(claps his shoulder)
Send me your check for the twenty thousand I asked for.

GEORGE
Thank you. Thank you...

WATSON
Don't mention it.

Watson exits, head proudly high, as George wanders back to slump behind his table. He barely has a chance to reach the desk when Masters (THE GIFT SHOP PROPRIETOR) enters, nattily dressed, carrying an artist's case containing large three-by-four-foot drawing cards.

MASTERS (gung ho)
Well sir, ready to see how the old empire is faring?

GEORGE
I suppose so, Masters.

MASTERS
(opens the case; sets up the
display on an easel)
A few little items here I thought we wouldn't want to miss, Mr. Hanley!

GEORGE
(wearily)
I thought I already owned one of just about everything made!

MASTERS
Ah ha ha, you can't keep up with Yankee ingenuity and productivity. We have to buckle down to some *serious* spending. We've got to keep you from having too much cash available, or the government's liable to invent a new tax bracket!
(displaying cards)
Now, here you have a handsome little yacht.

GEORGE
I have one already; ninety-four foot job up at Newport!

MASTERS
(glowing)
This one make it look like a dinghy. Isn't it handsome?

85.   CU PLACARD

The yacht looks like a rococo Queen Elizabeth.

86.   ANGLE ON GEORGE & MASTERS

GEORGE
(shakes his head)
You know, Masters, there's no fun in buying things anymore. Before I had money, I'd look forward to buying a second-hand car like a kid waiting for Christmas. Now there's no anticipation, no hungering. I just…write checks.

MASTERS
(reassuring)
You're feeling blue, Mr. Hanley.

GEORGE
(stares out the window)
I used to enjoy little things…an ice cream cone when it was hot; a ball game; getting out of the apartment for a walk in the park. Now, if I walk in a park, four people run up and ask me if I'm

>   going to subdivide it!
>   (to Masters)
>   I'm going to quit buying things!
>
>   MASTERS
>   (shocked)
>   That's…subversive!
>
>   GEORGE
>   You're nuts!
>
>   MASTERS
>   (impassioned)
>   It's un-American, Mr. Hanley! Salesmanship is
>   our way of life. Think of those men, living on
>   blue sky and a prayer, depending on *you* for their
>   daily commissions! They have little ones. Mouths
>   to feed. No, Mr. Hanley, you can't stop buying!
>   Never!
>   (shakes finger in his face)
>   Buying is your destiny! Don't waver now! Do
>   your duty, Mr. Hanley!

87.   OMIT

91.

92.   CU GEORGE IN HIS OFFICE

THE CAMERA MOVES TO REVEAL ROGER HACKETT WAVING HIS HAND IN HIS FACE TO ATTRACT HIS ATTENTION.

>   ROGER
>   Congratulate me…George, I said, congratulate me!
>
>   GEORGE
>   Congratulate you…?

Roger turns to address the office.

                    ROGER
           You're looking at the new head bookkeeper of
           this organization!

Ad lib congratulations from the staff, as Roger moves off on his next speech.

                    ROGER (CONT'D)
           Thank you, thank you. But the first thing I want
           to tell you guys is I intend to keep my vow. No
           more lousy lunches at Nick's!

93.   CU GEORGE

He is disgusted by the spectacle of Roger's success.

                    GEORGE
                 (to himself)
           Him! They gave it to him! He wasn't even a
           good chauffeur!

                                        FADE OUT.

                    ACT IV

       FADE IN:

94.   EXT STREET ANGLE ON GEORGE & ATTILA

George walks with his dog, the mutt trotting happily alongside his master, content simply to be in his presence. George has his hands thrust deeply into his pockets, pauses to sit on some deserted steps.

95.   FULL SHOT GEORGE & DOG

The animal instantly snuggles up to its master, full of affection.

                    GEORGE
                 (reflective)
           Well, we're down to the last choice, Attila. I'd
           never keep a beautiful wife; and money is no fun
           when you have everything. You just sit and look
           at it. Position, power, that's what makes the world

go round these days. Look at Mr. Watson giving
that job to Roger – believe me if I had power,
I'd be *fair*!
(a beat)
What do you think? Do I dare wish the third
thing...?

For answer, Attila only whines affectionately, but George leans back and begins to dream. The image shimmers as we

DISSOLVE TO THE DREAM

96.   EXT STREET WITH MOTORCADE (STOCK)

From an open car, a man standing in the rear, receives the adulation of the crowd. As it moves very slowly down the street, crowds press against the barriers, exultant. From the windows come a cascade of confetti, like the fabled porridge that wouldn't stop flowing from the pot.

97.   ANGLE ON CAR AGAINST SKY

And the man standing in the rear of the car, is President George Hanley, hair tipped with distinguished grey, affable, humble, a man of the people. He accepts the great cheers of the crowd with a sincere smile and little bows, first to one side, then to the other. In the seat beside him, a Secret Service man sits apprehensively. It is Sgt. Watson, concerned for his beloved leader.

WATSON
Sir, you'll be exhausted. Let me tell them to
hurry on to the airport.

PRESIDENT GEORGE
Watson, these people elected me; they respect me,
and they want to demonstrate their confidence.
They have placed in my humble hands, their
individual destinies. The least I can do is let them
see what kind of destiny they're getting!

WATSON
(passionately sincere)
They're getting the best, Mr. President. The best!

> PRESIDENT GEORGE
> (touched)
> Thank you; that means a great deal to me, coming from you.

DISSOLVE TO:

98. INT PRESIDENTIAL OFFICE DAY

(NOTE: THIS IS AGAIN THE PENTHOUSE SET, RE-DRESSED.)

Through partly opened drape, the glass windows reveal the Capitol Building, or the Washington monument. If inappropriate to the dignity of the office, we can dispense with the great seal and a flag, but they would be helpful. As a substitute we might use large portraits of Washington and Lincoln. There is a massive desk, and a very high-backed swivel chair, in which sits President George Hanley, frowning at a barrage of telephones. On one side is a huge photo of a hydroelectric dam and in front of it a lectern. On the lectern is a throw switch, the kind with a handle which is hinged to a base and connects with terminals if it is pulled down or up. Also, arrayed to one side are a group of men with attaché cases, plus a matronly secretary.

> GEORGE
> (into phone)
> I see…I see…I see. Then go ahead!

Hangs down, and immediately is confronted by one of the waiting men. George listens with one ear while signing papers.

> CONGRESSMAN
> Mr. President, this pension legislation will tear the party in two. If you let it come to the floor, I for one won't get a single vote in November from anyone over the age of ten!

> GEORGE
> Have you checked with the majority leader to see if he can kill it in committee?

> CONGRESSMAN
> No…I didn't ask him.

                        GEORGE
            Ask him. Tell him the President said to handle it.

Another phone lights up, and George listens as he beckons the next man in line. Throughout the scene he picks up phones, listens with half attention. All he ever says is "yes" or "no."

                        GEORGE
                        (in phone)
            Yes?...

                        WORRIED STRATEGIST
            The situation is fraught with tension in Asia,
            Mr. President. We're not getting enough
            intelligence down there!

                        GEORGE
                        (to phone)
            Hold on...Have the CIA prepare a full staff study.
            Tell Bill you need it right away.
                        (to phone)
            No!
                        (hangs up)

Second man leaves and the secretary thrusts a paper under George's nose.

                        SECRETARY
            Your appointments schedule, Mr. President.

                        GEORGE
                        (with charm)
            Thank you.

The third man approaches the desk, waits.

                        GEORGE (CONT'D)
            Move this press conference to after lunch. I need
            a haircut...I'll make the UN speech...have
            Lorenson whip a draft and remind him...jokes.

                        SECRETARY
            Yes, sir.

GEORGE
(points)
Who are Sonny and Mickey?

SECRETARY
Those cub scouts who wrote you the letter about citizenship...you asked to be reminded when they arrived in the capitol. I know there's no time.

GEORGE
Make time! We can get haircuts together.

SECRETARY
(nods and notes watch)
Almost ten o'clock Mr. President!

George nods, rises, heads for the drawing board.

GEORGE
(to last waiting man)
Pardon me, Murray.

He steps to the switch, notes his watch, waits for the exact second, and with vigor, pulls the switch. Then he turns, moves briskly back to the desk, with an air of accomplishment.

GEORGE (CONT'D)
Twenty million kilowatts for the people of the southwest! Too bad I can't make all these dedications in person!

George rubs his hands and attacks the pile, thrusting papers to the secretary and the assistant.

GEORGE
Pass this on to the Secretary of Defense...marked expedite... Save these for the Cabinet meeting... priority. Get the Economics Advisory Council to dig in on this!

SECRETARY
Yes, sir...right away, sir...

They exit, and George leans back, stretches his shoulders and sighs. What a busy morning he's having! He rises, heads for a small basket to one side, muttering to himself.

> GEORGE
> Decisions, decisions, decisions...eh Attila!

He scoops up a dog from the basket and returns to stare out of the big window toward the view. The dog in his arms is a small black animal of whatever breed Falla belonged to. Suddenly the long heavy drapes at the window, wiggle, betraying a human form behind them.

99.   ANGLE ON GEORGE

He reacts, thrusts Attila aside, then bravely yanks the drapes back to reveal a bent, grey-haired woman with a wrinkled face, and fearful eyes. It is Ann Lawson...older, plumper, dressed neatly but poorly, distraught.

> ANN
> (falling to her knees)
> Mr. President...I had to see you!

> GEORGE
> (startled)
> Who...what are you doing here, woman?

> ANN
> (hands clasped, pleading)
> I hid there. All night. It was the only way. They said you were too busy. Please listen to me. Don't send me away!

George hesitates an instant, then bends to help this woman to her feet, and let her rest in his own chair.

> GEORGE
> (sincerely)
> How can I help you?

                    ANN
           (tumbling out thru tears)
     It's...my son. He's just a boy...eighteen. He fell
     asleep on guard duty, and they said it was treason.
     They're going to hang him, Mr. President.
     Hang him!

                    GEORGE
     Easy, now. He's in the service, your boy?

                    ANN
     The Army. Special duty at a missile base.

                    GEORGE
           (gently)
     I see. Falling asleep on duty is very serious.

                    ANN
     Only a presidential pardon can save him! Please,
     sir. He's a good boy. Just a little tired! It could
     happen to anyone.

100.   FULL SHOT GEORGE

He studies her a moment, then draws himself to his full height.

                    GEORGE
     Indeed it could, ma'am.

101.   TWO SHOT

                    ANN
     Then you'll do it? You'll pardon him?

                    GEORGE
           (takes her hand)
     Ma'am...the world will not long remember what
     I say here, but this nation, the government...and
     its president, are no more and no less than people;
     of, by, and for them. If freedom is our battle cry,
     justice and mercy are our glory! You tell your son
     that, ma'am...when you see him tomorrow!

(lifts phone and barks into it)
Have the Attorney General prepare an order for executive clemency!
(hangs down)

The woman has risen, almost bows to him in reverence as she hurries out.

      ANN
    (in awe)
Thank you, thank you, thank you! You're a great man, Mr. President! Bless You!

She hurries out.

102. FULL SHOT GEORGE

He settles back in his oversize chair, scoops up Attila, ignoring the insistent intercom buzzer.

      GEORGE
Attila, I think we've found the right niche! Who ever said power was hard to handle? All you have to do is know how to use it!

103. ANGLE TO INCLUDE ENTRANCE

Before he can finish, the door bursts open and chairman of the Joint Chiefs, General Roger Hackett, zooms in, followed by three beribboned Chiefs of Staff and a civilian space expert. All are grim and tense.

      HACKETT
I couldn't wait, Mr. President. Those blips on the radar screens have just been identified: spaceships!

      SPACE EXPERT
From some strange planet.

104. FULL SHOT GEORGE

He almost chokes.

PRESIDENT
Spaceships? From another planet?

HACKETT
(nods)
Huge ones. Over a hundred of them.

PRESIDENT
...What do we do?

105. ANGLE ON GROUP

HACKETT
We can't take chances. Shoot them down!

SPACE EXPERT
You can't, Mr. President. There might be thousands of innocent people aboard.

George looks from one to the other, back and forth, as if watching tennis.

HACKETT
They're headed directly for us. We signaled them; they refused to answer.

SPACE EXPERT
It might be the greatest breakthrough of scientific investigation in the history of the universe.

HACKETT
If they're advanced enough to get here...think of their weapons! What they can do to us! Our only chance is to catch them with missiles before they arrive.

SPACE EXPERT
What if they're friendly?

HACKETT
What if they aren't?

                    SPACE EXPERT
          Let them land.

                       HACKETT
          Counterattack while there's still time.

                    SPACE EXPERT
          The decision is up to you, Mr. President. What
          do you say?

                        GEORGE
          How about a staff study…?

                        ROGER
          It's too late.

                        GEORGE
          Could we call in the cabinet…?

                        ROGER
          No time, sir!

                        GEORGE
          The Secretary of Defense…?

                        ROGER
          They'll arrive in minutes, sir. It's up to you!

106.   CLOSE UP GEORGE

Crumbling into panic.

                      PRESIDENT
          I can't. Let somebody else. I don't want to decide.
          Not me! Not me!

Abruptly his face blurs, the image whirls around, and the lamp is SUPERED, as we

                                    DISSOLVE THROUGH TO:

107.   EXT. STREET ANGLE ON GEORGE

He is mumbling to himself aloud.

                    GEORGE
            Not me! Not me!

CAMERA MOVES TO INCLUDE IRATE HOUSEOWNER IN SHIRTSLEEVES

                    HOUSEOWNER
            Yeah, you, Mac! You and your mutt get offa my
            stoop!

108.   FULL SHOT GEORGE

He grabs Attila and bustles off.

                    GEORGE
            Okay, okay.

109.   TRUCK SHOT

As George and Attila move down the street, then turn a corner.

                    GEORGE
            Come on, dog.

He plods off, Attila following

                                            DISSOLVE TO:

110.   INT GEORGE'S APARTMEMT

As they enter; George moves to stare at the lamp on its shelf.

                    GEORGE
            A magic lamp; anything I want, mine just for
            wishing it...and I can't even find what to wish for!
            I never thought it out before. It always seemed
            those three things were the best that could ever
            happen to a man!

Turns away, slumps in his chair.

                    GEORGE (CONT'D)
                (wryly)
            Know something, Attila? No matter what things
            I wish for, they won't change anything! I'm still
            me, George P. Hanley, vocation…jerk!
                (broods)
            What's the quotation…?

111.   CU GEORGE

Leans down to stare into Attila's tilted face.

                    GEORGE
                (mocking himself)
            "Men at some time are masters of their fates:
            The fault…"dear Attila"…is not in our stars,
                (bitterly)
            But in *ourselves!*…"

The dog whines reassuringly, licks his cheek.

                    GEORGE (CONT'D)
                (a sudden thought)
            Ourselves…!

112.   FULL SHOT GEORGE

He abruptly leaps up, runs and grabs the lamp, then returns with it excitedly, holds it nervous and tense.

                    GEORGE
                (to Attila)
            Get ready you bored, old Genie! We're going to
            wish for something…*original!*

CAMERA PUSHES IN TO THE LAMP AS GEORGE BEGINS TO RUB IT.

                                    MATCH DISSOLVE TO:

113.   EXT. ALLEY – CU ON THE LAMP – NIGHT

Lying on a heap of trash, but conspicuous. CAMERA PULLS BACK TO REVEAL THE SCENE, then we hear the sound of approaching footsteps; not stealthy or tipsy, but plodding. This is a man on his last legs.

114.   ANGLE ON DERELICT TO INCLUDE LAMP

He pulls one shoe off his tired feet and ruefully notes the sole. It has a large hole, and the man casts his eyes at the trash for something to stuff in it. He sees a piece of cardboard at hand and reaching for the cardboard notes the lamp.

115.   FULL SHOT DERELICT WITH LAMP

He picks it up, hefts it, turns it upside down, but finds nothing inside. He shakes it; still nothing. About to toss it away, he squints closer: it might be silver, so he rubs it against his tattered jacket and suddenly it seems to explode. In contrast to the percussion and restrained manifestations of the lamp before, this time it acts the way a magic lamp with a genuine Genie ought to act!

116.   CU LAMP

It glows with an unearthly light, there are repeated and deafening ROARS of thunder, then a blinding flash and the scene is obscured with billowing smoke.

117.   FULL SHOT MAN

He drops the lamp, shrinks back against the wall in fear and awe. Then he looks up, far up into the air, seeing an obviously astounding apparition. The apparition speaks from the depths of a multiple echo chamber.

                    VOICE
              (in proper, Genie style,
                drawn-out roar)
          Y…e…s, MMMaaasstteerr!

The man is stupefied.

118.   ANGLE ACROSS THE GENIE'S BACK

This is a real, old-fashioned, full of pizzazz, Genie. It wears a turban, pantaloons, naked above the waist: It is enveloped in a cloud of smoke: we can't see its face. (The voice should be sufficiently disguised to keep identification difficult.)

> VOICE
> I am the Genie of the lamp. Your wish is my command! You may have three wishes! But when you have made them, you must return the lamp to this alley where others will find it. At your service, sir.

119. FULL SHOT GENIE

The smoke swirls around him, but though turban is slightly askew, and the physique leaves something to be desired, we can see its beaming face, a smile of pure satisfaction lighting the familiar countenance of George P. Hanley. The Genie bends and picks something from the smoke at his feet: Attila yipping for pleasure, with a turban about his ears. George gives the assistant Genie an affectionate pet.

> SERLING'S V.O.
> Mr. George P. Hanley, former vocation…jerk: present vocation, Genie.

CAMERA PULLS BACK

> SERLING'S VOICE
> George P. Hanley, a most ordinary man whom life treated without deference, honor, or success; but a man wise enough to decide on a most extraordinary wish that makes him the contented, permanent master of his own, altruistic Twilight Zone.

FADE OUT.

THE END

AFTERWORD

As far as titles go, "Forgotten Gems from *The Twilight Zone*" is most appropriate for this collection.

The analogy of radiant, multifaceted and incredibly valuable stones certainly applies to *The Twilight Zone*. The series is a veritable treasure chest of imaginative and remarkably facile stories. And these tales have lost little of their sheen in the ensuing years. Given the transitory world of television entertainment, time has proved them to be as resilient and as rare as the Hope Diamond.

Various jewels are coveted not only for their beauty and rarity, but also for the unique properties they possess. Here too, the comparison holds. *Twilight Zone* scripts adhered to the guidelines of the series yet were as diverse and distinctive as the men who wrote them.

Millions of admirers are familiar with the cut, color and clarity of gems crafted by the series' major writers. Rod Serling mined the human psyche for clear, hard-edged diamonds-in-the-rough, which he shaped with precision chisel blows of social commentary and often displayed in tiffany settings of parable. Charles Beaumont bent the translucent, prismatic greens of the emerald to shape hypnotic stories that fused past with future and dream with reality. Richard Matheson seized on the bloodlike crimson of the ruby to carve horrors of lost identity and suburban nightmare. Earl Hamner and George Clayton Johnson peopled offbeat tales with rich, fanciful characters to add a number of smooth and shiny gemstones to the display.

But the writers above are not the sole suppliers of precious minerals. Several lesser-known authors provided scripts that add a sparkle of variation to the series.

Consider E. Jack Neuman's "The Trouble with Templeton," a touching story about a man's not-so-dead past and the specters who will not allow him to wallow in it. Or the chilling prospect of a woman so blinded by love and loneliness that she reaches from the beyond to expedite her grandson's demise, the premise of Bill Idelson's "Long Distance Call." Witness OCee Ritch's gritty underworld revenge tale entitled "Dead Man's Shoes," or the whimsically inept protagonist in John Furia's "I Dream of Genie," or "The Chaser," a breezy yarn about love and happiness and the occasional incompatibility of both, by Robert Presnell Jr.

Thanks to this collection, these stories—scattered throughout the display case of *The Twilight Zone* as decorative filler for so many years—can finally be examined and evaluated on their own merit. So break out your jeweler's eyepiece and hold them up to the light. I think you'll find that they shimmer with a beauty all their own.

- Tony Albarella

ABOUT THE EDITOR

ANDREW RAMAGE began his career as a television historian and researcher in the mid-1990's during his college years. *The Twilight Zone* and a number of comedy shows including *I Love Lucy, The Bob Newhart Show, The Andy Griffith Show,* and *All in the Family* were among the many shows he watched avidly for years while developing an appreciation for classic television. In 1999, he began what became a three-year project building the website MTMShow.com, an unofficial website on *The Mary Tyler Moore Show*. This led to appearances on radio station WCCO, Minneapolis, at the time of Mary Tyler Moore's statue dedication in 2002, and the first documentary release done on the show in 2001. He has also contributed to a number of books on classic TV and retro-TV documentaries, as well as the Lifetime Intimate Portrait™ of Cloris Leachman, one of his favorite actors. In 2002 and 2004, he hosted the "Stars of the *Twilight Zone*" Conventions in Hollywood. He maintains a historical tribute site to *The Twilight Zone* at TwilightZoneMuseum.com. Born, raised, and educated in Oregon, he holds a degree from the Linus Pauling Department of Chemistry at Oregon State University. He is also a classically-trained violinist. Mr. Ramage lives in Los Angeles, where he currently works as a documentary producer.

TONY ALBARELLA has chronicled *The Twilight Zone* series and the work of legendary writer Rod Serling in publications that include *Filmfax, Outré* and *Radiogram*. He is the co-author of "The *Twilight Zone* Scripts of Earl Hamner" and the editor of "As Timeless as Infinity: The Complete *Twilight Zone* Scripts of Rod Serling." He is a Board Member of The Rod Serling Memorial Foundation. He lives in New Jersey with his wife, Cindy, and his two daughters, Alyssa and Veronica.

BearManor Media

A bit of everything for everyone...
Television
Cinema
Radio

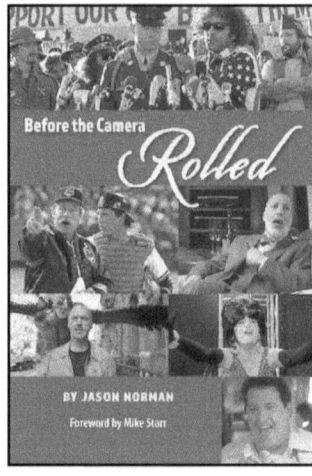

Hundreds of titles to check out!

www.bearmanormedia.com

www.ingramcontent.com/pod-product-compliance
Lightning Source LLC
Chambersburg PA
CBHW071433150426
43191CB00008B/1118